WHERE GOD BEGINS TO BE

Where God Begins to Be

A Woman's Journey into Solitude

Karen Karper

The biblical quotations that appear in this volume are taken from the New American Bible.

Originally published by Wm. B. Eerdmans Publishing Company

Copyright © 1994, 2004 by Karen Karper

ISBN: 978-1-5040-3696-2

Distributed in 2016 by Open Road Distribution
180 Maiden Lane
New York, NY 10038
www.openroadmedia.com

In loving memory of my hermit companion,
Merton the Tom,
and in gratitude to my many readers,
especially Paul, husband and friend,
who insisted that a second printing was essential.

There where clinging to things ends,
there God begins to be.

— MEISTER ECKHART

Contents

Introduction

HAVE you ever been seized by an impossible dream and then found yourself living into its fulfillment? *Where God Begins to Be* is the story of how I unexpectedly heard a call to live like the ravens and the lilies, trusting that a God who was enticing me to become a hermit in the late 1980s would lead me through mud to an occasional glimpse of glory.

Born in 1941, I was raised in a Catholic home through the tranquil 1950s. In 1959, when I was seventeen, I entered a monastery of Poor Clare nuns, expecting that this choice would determine the shape of my life until eternity dawned. Thirty years later I emerged from that same monastery to follow a dream of hermit life, seeking a form of poverty and a dimension of contemplative living that was not possible in a structured environment. This is the story of what happened when I went in search of my God and my soul at a time when the foundation of all I had built my life upon was shifting and cracking.

It was a foundation I had once deemed unshakeable. In an unchanging Church, the cloistered life seemed the most stable of all stable institutions. Within a fixed framework of prayer and silence, work and study, my novitiate began serenely enough. Even the bits of news that filtered in about the forth-coming Vatican Council did not portend any impact on my life.

1

I was taught and firmly embraced all the rules of living within the monastery and the four acres of trees and grass that made up our "enclosure." I was not to be concerned with what occurred on the other side of the pinkish block wall, beyond embracing it spiritually in prayer. I did not feel any contradiction in the practice of praying for a world about which I knew almost nothing.

And I didn't miss what I didn't know, because daily life within the monastery was full and interesting. I had my hours of private prayer during the day and two-hour stints on three nights of the week. In addition, I gathered with fifteen other sisters five times a day in the chapel to chant the official prayer of the Church, known then as the Divine Office.

My daily schedule included several hours of work in the kitchen, the laundry, or the altar bread department. I sewed habits and aprons, cleaned, and tended to whatever assignments were given me. After several years, I began to write poetry and reflections on the spiritual life that were occasionally published.

Twice daily I joined my sisters in the common room for conversation that was sprinkled with easy laughter. We discussed books we heard read in the refectory during meals, and the antics of the small wild creatures we observed on our grounds; we shared interest in one another's handcrafts; and we made plans for the various feasts and celebrations that generously studded the liturgical calendar which governed our daily life.

Once the Ecumenical Council opened in Rome in 1962, we were allowed to follow developments as recorded in the Catholic papers, and our conversations and interests were stimulated by larger concerns. Still, I made my profession of vows oblivious that this faraway event would create waves which would rock even the ancient vessel of Poor Clare life.

Liturgy, which intertwined our contemplative lifestyle, was one of the first areas of Catholic life to be addressed by the Council Fathers. When English replaced the venerable but little-understood Latin of the Mass and Divine Office, the framework of centuries of Poor Clare life began to tremble. It was the beginning of the end of an era — an inevitable ending of something beautiful that had grown and flowered but was now going to seed to make room for something new.

Intuitions of change and loss bore down on me. Dreams of earthquakes and chaos besieged my nights. I, along with my sisters, grappled with integrating fresh insights into ancient structures when further decrees mandated the renewal and updating of religious life itself. Medieval forms of dress were to be altered; penitential practices suitable to earlier ages were to be revised; and more communal participation in decision-making was to be introduced.

We began to realize that although the basic form of life we derived from Clare and Francis of Assisi was flexible enough to embrace the new wine of the Spirit now spilling abroad in the Church, the many rigid encrustations acquired through the eight centuries since their time was severely limiting that flexibility. Our challenge was to revive in the late twentieth century the fire that Clare and Francis had kindled in the thirteenth century, the fire of all-embracing love lived in poverty and humility.

I struggled to find my personal way within many conflicting interpretations of contemplative life. I did not believe those who claimed that contemplative communities would soon pass out of existence. Nor did I trust the voices which claimed that survival demanded clinging with blind fidelity to every tradition we had received.

Into my confusion drifted the siren song of solitude. It was a strange song to hear in the midst of the general call to a renewed sense of community that was sweeping through the Church. And I didn't want to hear it. For ten years, I successfully kept it in the background of my awareness.

I submerged myself in the work of renewal — the meetings, the rewriting of our Constitutions, the redefinition of enclosure and the practices of community life. But in the process, I grew more and more depressed. My health declined, and I was forced to spend many hours of the day alone in my room.

In that enforced solitude, I began to struggle with my sense of my own vocation as distinct from that of my sisters in the monastery. Desire for a wholeness that I intuitively sensed was possible but that I had not yet achieved despite years in a deeply prayerful community of dedicated women haunted me. Dimly I knew that only in solitude could I connect with the Source of my completion. It was frightening, and I might have dissembled forever had not my mother died in 1987, as well as another woman, an older nun who had been a mentor and a friend to me.

These two women had been models and teachers for me, not so much through their words (although their words of wisdom would be an enduring gift) as through their lives of faith and loyalty. Above all, it had been their belief in me which, like sunlight, had enabled me to see clearly my own gifts and strengths, and trust them. Suddenly these two women were gone, and at the age of forty-five, I was left with their mandate to grow into what they always knew I could be.

I learned to drive a car, something I had deliberately avoided doing because, frankly, I was afraid of what I might do with the independence it would afford me. Life was simpler when I *couldn't* do certain things. I was even spared dealing with the risk of an excursion into solitary living.

Tender traps can surprise the unwary. I was making a month-long retreat at a house of prayer when all sense of God's presence vanished for me. After several days of restless stalking of the grounds, I asked myself what precisely was happening. Immediately I had an image that I was standing at the end of a broad course where it branched into several smaller paths, and I was refusing to choose any one of them.

Very reluctantly, I began to explore seriously the call to solitude. My directors could do little more than listen with me and help me test the spirits. A providential opportunity to stay rent-free in a small place in West Virginia gave me a chance

4

to live alone for the first time in my life. After three months, I returned to the monastery to evaluate the experiment.

That time spent in the jerry-built house on the edge of a ravine had been difficult but profoundly revealing. I experienced the truth which Thomas Merton had written: that some people have to be alone before they can find their true selves. The loneliness of the first weeks gradually became a discovery of riches within my deeper self. I also recognized my innate need as a writer for the long periods of undisturbed quiet that encourage springs of creative inspiration to surface.

I began to define what "hermit life" meant for me. I was not called to be a recluse — that is, one who is cut off entirely from contact with others and "the world." This was neither practical nor desirable. I wished to maintain my affiliation with the nurturing community of my Poor Clare sisters, even though I felt called to live apart from daily interaction with them.

Contact with other hermits revealed to me that each one had developed a unique balance of solitude, work, and relationships. The ancient idea of the hermit who lived on the margins of society, separate but not cut off, who was available for spiritual counsel and occasional aid, appealed to me. I discovered that present-day hermits often had to define their daily lives not only by their dreams but by the means of livelihood available to them. Such would be true for me as well.

I felt compelled to search for a more permanent hermitage. I couldn't describe what I expected to find. The only guide I had was a tenuous thread winding me back toward some preconscious awareness of a time when I was wholly myself, wholly loved and loving, wholly *alive!*

A memory or a promise? It shimmered like a vision of a garden place with the sun rising out of morning mist and roses blooming on arched branches, while dew sparkled in the grasses. For this my spirit burned. I was seeking a place where the gate to the East might eventually open to me . . . if I were willing to wait.

Once I decided to move full-time into solitude, decisions

beyond my control forbade my return to the place of my original hermit experience. However, during those three months, I had made contact with two Franciscan sisters living in solitude and poverty in another part of West Virginia. Through them I learned of the house where I have lived for the past four years.

After four years, I am still waiting for that gate to the East to open. Perhaps, even after forty, I will be paraphrasing Robert Frost's poem: "I shall be telling you this with a sigh somewhere ages and ages hence — two roads diverged on an Appalachian ridge, and I took the steeper way, and my life has been forever different."

When I left the monastery in June 1989 to attempt solitary, contemplative life along that steeper way, I had no financial plan or backing. I had only a bargain I had struck with God. I would put first the requirements of contemplative living — the hours for prayer, reflection, for just "being." Whatever time might be left over, I would use to earn my keep. My only skills were sewing, writing, and spiritual direction — none of which is especially remunerative.

I would work as time and circumstances allowed. God would have to provide for the rest. The miracle of my story is that God has done exactly that, with a generosity beyond my wildest dreams. The ten-year-old Bronco and modest inheritance I started with are long gone — but I have yet to be without food, shelter, fuel, transportation, and other basic necessities.

Inexorably, the road I have chosen has turned, pitching me deeper into solitude and poverty than I would have dared to essay in my furthest fantasy. The way has been muddy and rocky, slippery when wet, and totally impassable when icy.

My witless adventure into solitude has proven to be a saga of divine Providence and, occasionally, of divine humor. I share with you some of the significant moments of this journey, which has given me, among other things, a great appreciation for a pair of stout boots.

I

The Road Once Taken

Two roads diverged in a yellow wood, . . . and I —
I took the one less traveled by,
And that has made all the difference.

Robert Frost, "The Road Not Taken"

IN ACTUAL fact, the woods weren't yellow — they were May green and drooping in a downpour. The "less traveled road" wasn't leaf-covered but deeply rutted, steep, and muddy. And I traveled it not on foot but clinging to the dashboard of a bouncing pickup . . . and I had doubts that even if I arrived at the end, it would make any difference. I only intended to make a courtesy call on some friends and then escape this alien and appalling terrain.

With the help of a sister-friend, I had just packed up my Bronco and said farewell to the little place on the edge of a mountain in West Virginia where I had spent the past three months testing my call to solitude. I was on my way back to the monastery in Ohio, but I had decided to accept an invitation from two Franciscan sisters, Jeanne and Jane, to visit their isolated dwelling place in an Appalachian valley called Colt Run holler. Through a chain of mutual acquaintances, Jane and Jeanne had learned of me, and I had heard of them through various correspondents. So when Jeanne phoned me during my three-month trial period, I had gladly invited her and Jane to visit me. Now I was paying a return call.

Forewarned by Jeanne, who had navigated the descent into this holler for eleven years, I had not attempted to drive my heavily laden Bronco down off the ridge. Instead, I had parked on the edge of the narrow road and waited with my friend for Jeanne to taxi us down in her four-wheel-drive pickup.

The track she had turned onto appeared to pitch perilously over the edge of the ridge, but Jeanne seemed unperturbed as the truck bounded over ruts and rocks. I got a blurred impression of overhanging trees through the streaming windows and glanced at my friend, who was crouched in the tiny space behind the front seat. Her grim jaw and my white knuckles spoke volumes. Then my head hit the roof as we lurched around yet another wicked turn.

Jeanne waved toward my right, telling me to notice a house situated below. I peered through the mist and foliage but could see nothing. What sort of house could be situated down there? I did glimpse a collapsing barn, one of the many abandoned structures I had noticed dotting the Appalachian countryside at depressing intervals.

To my relief, the truck hit flatter ground, and soon we pulled up by a small house with a weathered front porch. However much I felt attracted to living my future hermit life in the woods, this descent into Colt Run holler convinced me it would not be here.

There was seclusion and then there was sheer insanity. To choose to live where access was so dangerous was obviously the latter. Jane, who apparently shared Jeanne's courage and vision, welcomed us as she bustled about the kitchen, shouting cheerfully over the steady thrum of rain on the tin roof. The road was particularly bad, she explained, because of the rains of recent weeks. I listened abstractedly — it didn't really concern me personally.

The four-room cabin that was the center of Jeanne and Jane's modest arrangements had electricity and a phone. However, the wood stove in the center of their front room seemed a dubious attraction, and the wringer-washer on the back porch shocked me. On that day, pans were set about in strategic places where the roof was leaking (which it only did when it rained, Jane assured me with a grin).

After a lunch of grilled cheese sandwiches, garnished with alfalfa sprouts, and berries picked in the woods the previous day, Jane and Jeanne took my friend and me on the Grand Tour. I gingerly picked my way along muddy paths and across boards that spanned small runs (the seasonal streams that abound there). Their chapel deep in the woods was a rustic structure paneled with old barn siding.

Jeanne's hermitage, even further into the woods, featured a large loom and a sleeping loft. No electricity reached these simple buildings. The sound of rain and the music of myriad birdcalls enhanced the silence.

Jane's place of retreat was an old smokehouse remodeled as a pottery, where she produced beautiful wares that contributed to their very modest income. She proudly led us up a slippery path to their guest hermitage, a tiny building surrounded by trees and furnished with a sleeping platform, a built-in desk, and an old rocker.

Coming and going through the wet woods, we passed and repassed the inevitable outhouse, one of the few such structures I had encountered in my sheltered life. My middle-class upbringing in a university town had never exposed me to physical hardships of the kind I observed were part and parcel of life in this rural setting. Although I was used to the austere poverty of the monastery, it did not include the material deprivations that lack of indoor plumbing implied. Even as I trekked in

9

borrowed boots about this new terrain, a host of contradictory feelings assailed me.

I loved the woods; I hated the mud. I felt healed by the silence; I feared the deprivation of modern conveniences. I marveled at the vigor of these two women, who had built most of these structures with their own hands; I was keenly aware of my own physical limitations. I spontaneously responded to the wild beauty of the place; I trembled when copperheads entered the conversation.

Back at the cabin, my friend and I listened curiously as Jane entertained us with her dulcimer. Mateo, their blind cockapoo, panted at my feet, while Julian, their grey tabby, twined lovingly about my legs. Something mysterious was happening to me, something that made me suspect a hidden trap. Suddenly I was eager to get on the road, headed back to the safe, familiar, and clean environment of the monastery.

When Jeanne drove my friend and me back up to the ridge, I felt admiration but no attraction to a place where mud and risk were facts of daily life. If anything, the harrowing drive up the steep hill confirmed all my fears. As I unconsciously leaned forward to help the spinning wheels find traction and avoid the deeper ruts, all my survival instincts flashed warnings.

Only after we attained the interstate an hour later did I begin to relax and admit all the contradictory emotions that had crowded those brief hours in Colt Run holler. "Country roads, take me home" . . . but not *that* country road, please God! Yet the mystical sense of coming home created by the dripping green leaves, the trailing veils of mist, the silence, and the solitude would not leave me. And the house I had not seen among the tangled foliage haunted me.

As we drove along, a sinking realization dawned — I had taken a road that day which would, as Robert Frost wrote, "make all the difference." It was an unwanted road and yet one which, I sensed, could lead me into greater fulfillment than any

I dared to imagine. The profound, irresistible drawing to solitude with which I was grappling had imperatives of poverty and marginal living that I had not recognized before.

In this hidden valley, in an almost forgotten part of North America, I was being called to find springs of healing and peace, which might, in time, become a gift to many. I was hearing an invitation that I sensed would not only shatter the shape my life had taken for the past thirty years but also demolish my image of myself. This was not an attractive prospect, and I declined the invitation. Or so I thought.

Once back at the monastery, I busied myself searching for a hermitage. The few options available dwindled to none. Then I received a note from Jane. The house up the road from theirs was about to be vacated. She and Jeanne knew the owner, now living out of state, and thought he could be persuaded to let me live there rent-free in exchange for upkeep.

This suggestion was the only door now open to me. I mentally waved the letter before God's nose and stormed about high-handed tactics. Did I detect a celestial chuckle? My capitulation was less than gracious. Colt Run holler would do only until I could find something more suitable.

Thus, mid-June of 1989 found me in my worn-out Bronco, shakily turning down into the dreaded, enchanting holler again. Along with some clothing and a few hundred dollars, I had my Bible, a typewriter, and quilting hoops. Together with the Bronco, they constituted all the assets I had with which to establish and maintain myself as a hermit in the "real world."

No one thought I would be able to make it for long. I myself had no assurance other than that which Jesus gave in the Scriptures: "Seek first [God's] kingship over you, his way of holiness, and all these things will be given you besides" (Matt. 6:33).

As a Franciscan, I had been brought up to believe that God would provide for all my needs, but I had never really put this faith to the test. Life in the monastery was secure and

11

relatively comfortable in its simple way. It had tradition and canonical approval behind it. Hermits, on the other hand, were suspect and not particularly welcome in most dioceses. Three bishops, in fact, had informed me that they did not want me living as a hermit within their jurisdictions.

The major reason for this, I inferred, was monetary. No one wanted to be financially responsible for me. But I had not asked them for material support — only permission to live in solitude. That a woman lacking experience in the practical details of survival could live a contemplative life as a hermit and not be financially dependent on others did not occur to them.

If the authorities had asked me how I thought this could be done, I could not have answered them. All I had to cling to was the Gospel stories about the birds of the air and the lilies of the field. It was these texts that had inspired St. Clare, in the year 1212, to leave her family home and begin a life of total dependence on God at San Damiano outside the walls of Assisi.

Bishops hadn't believed her either when she claimed that God would provide all she needed if she only sought first the Kingdom. I had walked through Clare's life, hand in hand with her, as I wrote the pages of her biography. Together we had met Francis, who was taking the Gospel literally and discovering delirious joy in the freedom that total dispossession of all worldly goods gave him. Clare had chosen to walk off the edge of the cliff of material security along with Francis, and the world of her day had been so dazzled by her decision that by the time of her death, one hundred and fifty monasteries of women were walking onto the thin air with her.

Clare had chosen a place literally outside the mainstream of civilized life in the thirteenth century, rejecting status, security, and approbation. Now she seemed to be riding with me as I bumped and slid to a stop before my new neighbors' cabin in Colt Run, and Jeanne and Jane ran out crying, "Welcome home!"

12

II

Little House in a Holler

SCREWDRIVER in one hand, a can of WD-40 in the other, Jeanne scurried up the long drive with me on a sticky July day. As we strode past towering weeds, she muttered about unreliable people who promise to leave keys behind and then drive off, taking them to another state.

A month had passed since I had arrived in Colt Run, a month of rain and mud, during which I had waited impatiently at the guest hermitage at Jeanne and Jane's place while the family up the road — living in what I had begun to think of as "my house" — got their vehicles running, their possessions together, and their plans implemented for a move out of West Virginia.

"This may not work," Jeanne said darkly, as we approached the weathered house sheltered under huge pines. A narrow walk curved toward the steps leading up to the front door I had tried unsuccessfully to open for the past hour. Dilapidated as the house appeared, the front door, stoutly padlocked, was formidable. Low and wide, four inches thick, this door had defeated my every effort to enter this Appalachian cabin I was hoping to turn into a hermitage.

The former tenants had pulled out that morning, promising to leave the key in the mailbox up on the ridge. I had made the twenty-minute trek up the now-familiar hill, only to dis-

13

cover that the key was not there — or anywhere else. With my frustration peaking, I tramped back to Jeanne and Jane's place to explain my dilemma.

Jeanne wasted no time gathering the requisite tools, and soon we were trotting up the dirt road that separated the two houses in Colt Run holler. Together we faced the enemy. The weathered door, with its padlock gleaming maliciously, defied us as we tried first one key and then another.

Finally, a few squirts of WD-40 and an expert twist of the Phillips screwdriver loosened the entire lock from the door frame, and the door swung heavily inward. I stepped over the threshold and took a deep breath — which I immediately regretted. Cats and mice had cohabited with the former tenants, and their presence was evident! I looked about apprehensively, noting faded calico tacked along the lower half of the living room walls. "What's behind that?" I asked.

"Nothing but studs," Jeanne responded. "The fellow who remodeled this place planned to build a couch around the walls. . . . Left the state before finishing the job," she added vaguely while kicking at the rippled carpeting.

I considered the rough redwood (?) boards set in a diagonal pattern along the upper walls. "Creative," I murmured, not realizing then just how flimsy "artistic" construction could be.

A piano leaned against one wall, its yellowed and broken keys predicting how wretchedly out of tune it was. It was the only piece of furniture in the room except for a velvet armchair of indefinable color.

I turned toward a windowed alcove. A low table surrounded by a built-in bench reminded me of an Oriental tearoom. The odor was stronger here, and I noticed stains on the sloping ceiling. It had been casually mentioned that the ceiling leaked whenever it rained. . . .

A rumbling vibration startled me, and I stared in awe as the old refrigerator, graciously left for my use, kicked into action.

14

"Oh, God!" Jeanne exclaimed. "How can anyone live with that kind of noise?"

I was about to respond when the pump under the kitchen sink began to whine, something it did at twenty-minute intervals because of a slow leak somewhere in the line. I swung open the cupboard that caged the pump, and my heart dropped when I noticed rotting wood beneath the holding tank. The aroma of mold was strong. The stained sink and blackened countertops appalled me, and I reeled back, bumping into a table that had also been left for me, albeit without any chairs. Jeanne's lips were moving, and I could guess what she was saying even without hearing the words.

Continuing my exploration, I wandered into a dark bathroom. A rust-stained tub was sunk into one corner. Near it stood a homemade potty with a bucket beneath. A sink in another corner appeared to have been unused for the past century, and I guessed why when I noticed that it had no connecting drain. White plastic pipes ran around the walls.

"There is running water," I comforted myself. Little did I suspect what grief that water would cause me.

The surrounding walls next caught my attention. Inlaid woodwork clearly depicted a sunrise over the mountains. Another wall was decorated with a cunning mandala arranged by an artist whose imagination had exceeded his carpentry skills.

"There is probably no other bathroom like this in West Virginia," Jeanne observed.

"Truly!" I echoed fervently.

Near the bathroom door, irregular steps wound up a corner to a loft bedroom. "What next?" I wondered as I grabbed the bannister of two-by-fours. I blinked as I climbed into a sun-drenched room of gracious proportions paneled with knotty pine. A sloping ceiling with dark beams added to the surprising charm of this loft.

15

"I can write here!" I exclaimed as I gazed about at the built-in shelves, the floor-to-ceiling windows opposite each other, and the green vista they framed. For reasons I could not immediately define, I sensed that I had stepped into a space in which my spirit could be both contained and set free. Whisperings of future developments reached my inner ear, and I nodded in unspeakable satisfaction. It was so right!

I had always been influenced by my environment, especially when it came to writing. In small, cramped quarters, I seemed unable to write. Noise and clutter also distracted me. But here was a room filled with warm light, inviting, friendly, slightly above the demands of daily necessities. This empty loft evoked poetry and teased me to explore my inner rooms.

Despite the many challenges of occupying this unfinished house, I felt confirmed that here I could, like St. Clare at San Damiano, "fix the anchor of my soul." Unexplored vistas shimmered in the very air, and I could hardly wait to get to my typewriter, although where I would set it was a moot question.

I assessed this loft room, dominated by a built-in double-bed frame. The carpeting up here smelled fresher even though the heat of the July day was trapped under the low ceiling. The closet door lay on the floor. The closet itself was amazingly large. Only later did I learn that I shared it with a squad of flying squirrels.

Through a back window the rusting roof of a shed was visible. It added to the Appalachian atmosphere, in company with two stoves that lurked in the weeds and an old freezer that stood in the open cellar along the north side of the house. Thoughtfully I descended the steps, passing the mural of a soaring multicolored bird, another legacy of the free spirit of the former tenant.

With Jeanne's help, I undertook the task of rolling up the rug in the front room and heaving it outside. Then we tackled the odorous situation in the alcove. As we pulled the table loose and pried up the bench (both had been nailed to the floor),

Mama Mouse scurried by with a baby in her mouth. We found the nest and conveyed the rest of the litter outdoors. I was blissfully unaware that this was only one of several families who shared my house.

My young cat showed only mild interest in his housemates, an attitude I hoped would soon change. He was carrying the vision of the Peaceable Kingdom, where the cat would lie down with the mouse, further than I was prepared to go!

I spent the next few days with scrub brush and scouring powder, liberally augmented with elbow grease. My first priority was to create a personal clean space within the house. That the wilderness outside threatened to come inside and harbored unwanted denizens didn't matter for the moment. It was the denizens within that concerned me.

Moving into a new house was like putting on a new skin. And donning a new skin implied shedding the old one, a painful process that threatened to leave me somewhat shapeless and vulnerable for an indefinite period of time. I sensed that the form my future life took would be determined by my choice of a dwelling place . . . and what I would allow to live there. I brought many unwanted critters with me — fear, distrust, anger, grief, resentment. Some I was already aware of; others would be revealed only in the stark discipline of solitude.

The dawning recognition that I was being called to change not only where and how I lived but also the why's and wherefore's of my living was terrifying. It was like looking into a mirror and seeing my self-image dissolve into formless mist. Many faces appeared and disappeared, few of which I wished to own as mine. Yet I knew they were all parts of me that I had to meet and welcome.

Like the house itself, I felt so very unfinished yet brimming with potential, designed by Someone with visions and dreams. The challenge of realizing those dreams, of giving concrete shape to powers and gifts freely bestowed on me, was daunting.

17

No one could show me my true face. Only I, with grace, could find the way to become a reflection of my Dreamer.

Despite its multiple problems, this house felt strangely right. It was large enough to give me a sense of inner space and isolated enough to provide an atmosphere of solitude. It was a place that I could slowly "live into," letting it put its imprint on me even as I gradually put the stamp of my dreams on it. I had a haunting sense of having stumbled into a sacred grove where the Holy had been worshiped, where a search for mystical experience had been conducted.

This sense of the pneuma that pervaded the place spoke to the deepest longings of my spirit. For I had made this mad leap out of the security of contemplative life in the monastery into solitude because I sensed that only in solitude would I experience the wildness of the New Age aborning in the church; only in solitude could I develop a vision wide enough to embrace this wondrous new child with the compassion that an infant requires.

Such compassion could be discovered only in prayer. One of my first interior decorating projects was to set up a worship space in the windowed alcove from which the mice family had been evicted. Jane helped me reconstruct the low bench into a slightly raised platform that I covered with a donated piece of lavender carpet — a "mystical color," Jane assured me.

On it I placed a wood table-altar and plant stand, handmade by a friend. A cushion completed the furnishings, while a jar of wildflowers added a grace note. Through the windows I could see the giant pines that shaded the patchy yard near the house and the ridges that rose steeply on either side, giving me a sense of protection I sorely needed.

The first evening that I could settle into prayer in my new worship space, my eyes were drawn to the living room wall opposite. Yes, indeed, fading daylight shone between the rough boards! Though I was definitely interested in fresh visions, I was not prepared for transparent walls! I studied the situation more closely and realized that not only was there no insulation, but there was neither siding nor shingles on the entire north side of the house.

This explained why the living room ceiling dripped whenever it rained even though the bedroom was directly overhead. Water apparently ran down the outside of the house and across a beam. Dismay filled me, because I had no money for major repairs.

Another source of distress sat along this same north wall — that piano! I had just barely been able to pull the ratty carpeting out from under it. Its very ugliness depressed me. How, in God's name, could I get it *out*? I pondered the possibility of axing it up for firewood.

A few days later, as I was applying a coat of enamel to the kitchen sink, a truck rattled up my drive. Four men and a boy jumped out. "We've come to pick up the piano, Ma'am," they announced politely. I asked no questions as I indicated the hulk in the corner. Scarcely believing, I watched as they wrestled it through the door and onto the truck.

The old piano, symbol of all the insuperable tasks facing me, departed down the drive and up the steep track to the ridge. I seemed to hear a still, small Voice inquire, "Is anything impossible with God?" Suddenly I *knew* that no matter how formidable life might seem, there would always be a way to deal with it.

This experience of Providence proved prophetic as help arrived from various and unexpected quarters. Cousins appeared on the scene with the building supplies and the skills needed to make emergency repairs before the winter winds set in. Members of the parish donated furniture. My cupboards filled with donated canned goods and other staples that insured I would eat well for months to come. A couple befriended me and gave me a small washer-dryer purchased with money they

19

had begged from others. A cousin in the carpeting business donated remnants that not only covered the floor but also replaced the calico on the walls, providing needed insulation.

When Jeanne and I tracked down a wood stove for sale but discovered that it was far too heavy for the two of us to load onto her pickup, three husky men materialized who not only loaded the stove onto the truck but came with us to set it in place by my chimney. Jeanne and Jane taught me the art of making a wood fire and helped me collect a winter's fuel supply.

By November, my initial fears about moving into a primitive place in Appalachia were allayed. Someone, whose dreams for me were larger than any I dared to entertain, had taken charge of my life and every detail of it. All that was asked was that I trust and take the next step into the dark. As the saying goes, when there is no solid ground under your feet, you will be taught to fly. And flying can be fun, I discovered!

Deep content and gratitude bubbled up in my heart, along with an increasing sense of security. Although threats to survival were all around me and my future was precarious, Love upheld me as an eagle her young.

Freely I delighted in the quaint beauties, the rough loveliness, the unique character and grace of this little house in a holler that I christened "Beth Shalom," House of Peace. My peace would be threatened frequently in the months and years ahead, but for the moment, I rested in wonder at the Love that had brought me thus far.

The huge pines stood guard like veiled women, blunting the winds and sifting the first of the winter snows. No longer was I an alien in a strange and hostile place, for I had found the doorway to my true home in this shabby, charming house of promise.

III

Floods of . . . Grace

A S USUAL, this morning was not forecasting one of those routinely quiet days I'd fondly envisioned when I had planned my move into a hermitage. Water squished between my toes as I danced vigorously on the dozens of rags and towels spread over the wet carpeting. A flood pouring through the bathroom door had jerked me away from my meditation on (of all things!) "Launch out into the deep" (Luke 5:4). Suddenly the deep was launching into me, and I sprang into panicked action.

This flood could not even be called an act of God, as most West Virginia floods were, but merely the result of my own stupidity. The previous night I had poured a half-gallon of chlorine bleach down the well to disinfect the holding tank and pipes. Intending to flush it through the system, I'd turned on the tub faucets and failed to notice that the plug was in place.

As I wrung out rags and rolled back carpeting to expose wet floorboards to the fan, I lamented the loss of the fresh morning hours that I liked to devote to writing. My daily life seldom seemed to follow the contemplative rhythm that others assumed I was enjoying.

It was nearly noon by the time I'd done two washer-loads of dirty rags and throw rugs and hung them on lines to dry in

21

the hot sun. As I tried to settle in for a bit of midday reflection, the phone rang. It was Jack, an old-timer from up on the ridge, who took a special interest in his "baby dolls" who lived in the holler.

I listened patiently as he described the condition of his apple crop (deers was eatin' 'em); his riding lawnmower (the left hind wheel was flat agin); and his "artheritis" (terrible). He chuckled gleefully as I described my morning flood and helpfully advised I don' do it no more. Agreed!

Hanging up the phone, I thought about how totally aware of all the minutiae of his environment Jack seemed to be. He'd call to describe a pair of titmice building a nest in "his" birdhouse or to tell me about the swarm of red ants in his yard. A few weeks earlier, he'd told me about the squirrel that had been stunned by a passing car in front of his house.

Jack had picked it up off the road; its eyes were rolling in its head, where a huge bump was forming. He'd put the frightened creature in a box and dribbled water into its mouth, then left it in a protected corner near his barn. To his delight, a few hours later the squirrel had recovered enough to stagger sideways down the hill. The next day Jack had seen it scampering through his trees, misshapen head and all.

Jack apprised me of the state of his roses (which the deers also nibbled) as well as his ongoing battle with the Japanese beetles. The white skunks that traipsed through his back lot occasioned advice on how to catch them without getting sprayed. You grab them by the tail, he told me, and keep their forefeet off the ground.

Jack could look at any piece of wood and tell you what it was — shagbark hickory, white or black oak, chestnut or cherry. He instructed me on what would burn fast or long, hot or slow. He had lived close to the land of his native ridges, and though he was unable to read a book, he read the face of nature in all her seasons with astute insight. From him I was learning about living with awareness, about observing small phenomena and finding pleasure in the simplest events. Even a ruined morning did not seem quite so catastrophic within the larger scheme of nature surrounding me.

My day had begun tranquilly enough at 5:30 A.M. with a clear summer sky promising another hot one. I spent my prayer time thanking God for the peace and beauty of the holler in summer. Around 7:30 I had wandered outside, savoring the lingering coolness. My house, barely visible under the dark pines, assumed a mystical aura in the sunrays slanting through the mist.

It all seemed doubly wonderful because I had just returned from leading a weeklong retreat on St. Clare at a retreat house in Ohio, and I was glad to be home. I agreed to do such workshops three or four times a year in order to generate some needed income, but I carefully spaced them so I could maintain the essentially solitary thrust of my life.

In truth, I hated to ever leave the hermitage and often wished I had the gift of bilocation so that I could go on with my "real" life in the holler even when I was away. I acknowledged an irrational anxiety that one day I would leave this little house and be unable to return or would come back to find it vanished into the mist, like Avalon.

Now I tried to calm my frustration and collect my thoughts as I ate my lunch of yogurt and an apple on the front porch. I caught sight of a flock of wild turkeys picking and pecking their way up my drive and realized that my feelings were as skittish as they.

That afternoon, as I was working at some machine quilting, I heard an ominous rumble from over the ridge and noticed that the sun had darkened. I darted out into the rising wind to take the now-dry rags and rugs off the lines. My cat, Merton, his fur bristling as lightning crackled, raced through the door ahead of me and took refuge under the bed for the duration of a wild summer storm.

The run beside the house rose swiftly, brown with runoff, as, fifty feet above me, water cascaded from a culvert under the road. The heavy downpour kept me checking the pans set in strategic places, especially around the chimney, which thrust through the upstairs closet. Despite my best efforts to keep things dry, a rain always increased the rank odor of mildew in the house. The soggy carpets would only contribute to the problem, I feared.

By late afternoon, the rain had subsided, and humming-birds were once more zooming about the feeder outside my kitchen window. Merton emerged from napping under the bed and set out to re-establish his claim to the dripping land.

I put aside the sewing that contributed to the bit of steady income I could earn at home and returned to my worship space for some quiet time with the Lord. As I fingered my breviary, I thought of my sisters in the monastery, who would also be going to Evening Prayer at this hour. I felt very close to them, although I saw them only about once every two months.

These brief visits helped me to maintain my bonds of love and friendship with my sisters, as well as a legal tie with the community. "I am who I am today because of the years I spent with these nuns," I mused. Thomas Merton had commented on the wise Benedictine tradition that allowed a monk to move into solitude only after spending twenty years in community living.

I appreciated the truth of this ancient dictum. My years in the monastery had trained me in prayer, stretched my capac-ity to love, and taught me the necessity of a contemplative routine. I had also learned how to adjust to constant shifts in that rhythm when the unexpected routinely occurred.

I generally reserved my evening hours for outdoor tasks such as weeding the flowers or mowing the lawn with an heir-loom machine that required neither gas nor oil, only push-power. With the sun sinking behind the western ridge, these were pleasant chores in the summer twilight.

But this evening it was too wet to work outside, so I contented myself with the twenty-minute hike up the road to the mailbox on the ridge. My reward was a red, white, and blue envelope stamped "Extremely Urgent." The flip side assured me that I was one of the lucky winners in a million-dollar cash giveaway if. . . . I shook my head, bemused that, even here, sweepstakes literature invaded with its gaudy offers of Caribbean cruises and Lincoln Continentals. Who needed these? Certainly not someone like Jack, who had spent his life contentedly watching the sun rise and set over these ridges and hollers.

Descending the hill, I pondered how rich I already was. The fragrance of sweet clover filled the air, and briars hung heavy with shiny blackberries, newly ripened. I glimpsed a red fox crossing the road ahead of me as well as an indigo bunting on a nearby branch. Water from the afternoon shower still gurgled in the ditch where peepers shrilled. I heard the bullfrog's whumping from a hidden pond, and the eerie hoot of an owl.

Later, I sat on the porch watching the fireflies begin their sparkling dance while I awaited the return of Merton, the Mighty Hunter. I reviewed the day, which had been unlike any other. Each event, welcome or not, had been an invitation to awareness, a moment of grace. Indeed, there had been veritable floods of grace for which to be thankful once again.

IV

Perpetual Muddy Boots

LEANING against each other or lying prostrate, gaping mouth to toe, or simply bent over like broken reeds, boots line the porch. Four pairs of them, all mine, all muddy. From November through April, boots are "de rigueur" once I descend the porch steps. They vividly depict the messiness of real life in Colt Run holler and offer some feeble defense against it.

Beside them, Merton, my white cat, lifts a hind leg over his head as he carefully grooms his immaculate fur. He has just come in from a romp in the mud; it is clumped on my boots, but only a minuscule fleck of dirt clings to his fluffy coat.

"How do you do it?" I marvel for perhaps the thousandth time. Merton looks up at me with inscrutable golden eyes and then returns to the meticulous work on his backside.

The June that I arrived in Colt Run was the rainiest on record. For several weeks I stayed in the guest hermitage at Jeanne and Jane's place, until I could move to the house that was to be my permanent dwelling. During my first visit I had briefly inspected this tiny building. Now it became my place of initiation into hermit life in the woods. It was here that I discovered *mud* . . . pervasive, perpetual, prophetic.

In order to reach this hermitage, I had to cross a plank over a gurgling run and climb a slick track around emerging

27

rock formations. The path struck into the woods at a vertical pitch that caused me heart palpitations by the time I reached my new abode, situated five hundred feet above the main house.

Trekking up this muddy path with trees dripping coolly around me demanded grit; descending the slick course required courage and more than a measure of divine favor. The red clay of Colt Run is devilishly treacherous when wet — and leaves its indelible mark. Within my first week, my shoes and socks were stained beyond redemption, even by bleach or Grandma's Lysol.

Wherever I went — the kitchen in the main house, the chapel in the deep woods, the outhouse — I learned to pull on boots and slop through mud, taking either a raincoat or an umbrella along. Invariably, whenever I would venture forth without rain gear, heaven would open its floodgates. Too often I found myself caught in the chapel while a new storm swept through the surrounding trees. As the pattering on the tin roof increased to a drumming, I would ruefully recall the boots or umbrella sitting in the hermitage at a wet and muddy distance.

And I would ask again, Why, oh why, had I come to Colt Run? It was the strangest place I had ever lived, remote from most of the conveniences I was accustomed to and abounding with forms of nature I had never wished to know so intimately. My sense of who I was began to erode. I felt like a swimmer beyond her depth . . . but can you swim in mud?

The guest hermitage was equipped with broom and bucket, which I intended to utilize in my struggle to keep the mud at bay. But I discovered that all water had to be toted painfully up the path and was, therefore, too precious to be used for more than essentials. I found my tactics inexorably shifted from scrub-bing the floor to waiting until the mud had dried enough to be swept outside — along with the bodies of wasps and roaches, which I condemned to untimely deaths whenever I could.

I nearly came to an early end myself, because I failed to

heed Jane's warning about providing for sufficient ventilation when I used the Coleman lantern at night. The mere process of lighting this volatile lantern terrified me, and I would be trembling by the time I had the air flow and wick adjusted for a flame bright enough to read by. One cool evening, I found myself woozy and ill. . . .

An angel reminded me of Jane's admonition, and I flung open windows to chill and rain and tiny buzzing critters as well as saving fresh air. It was a tribute to my devotion to reading and writing during the dusky hours of evening that I conquered my fear of the Coleman and kept the windows open, learning to disregard gnats and millers and brave the cool night air, bundled up in a sweater and knit cap.

The mud mirrored my inner state too exactly for me to find it anything but totally distressing. My spirits were shrouded in gloom as I endured the grieving, the anger, the recurrent panic about the future that assailed me during this period. That Jane and Jeanne were taking all this mud cheerfully in stride did not comfort me. They acted like this was *normal!*

One rainy afternoon as I slumped in the chapel feeling only alienation and loneliness, I distinctly heard, "You must lose all that you have become until now in order to become all that you really are." Although this was not a consoling insight, it afforded some frame of reference for the chaotic sense of loss I was experiencing. I clung to it as a drowning person to a rock.

I had worked hard to achieve the measure of integration and success in living that had been mine in the monastery. But that self was not the sum total of what I was created to be. It had become too constricting. The shedding of that self made me feel very, very vulnerable. Was my new "shape" to be made visible only through the mud splashed on it?

One day when both Jeanne and Jane were away, I enjoyed the luxury of a bath and shampoo in the main house. This was a hard-earned luxury, because the tub had to be filled with water heated in buckets on the stove. Afterward I slipped into fresh clothes and reveled in the simple joy of cleanliness. For once it wasn't raining, and there was a hint of sunshine. The fragrance of wild roses drifted from the damp woods.

After filling a milk jug and a bucket from the outdoor spigot, I started up the path to the hermitage. Mateo, Jeanne and Jane's blind but lively white dog, leapt about my feet, and Julian, their cat, wound about my legs. I wasn't wearing boots and didn't realize how slippery my old tennies were. Thanks to the antics of Mateo and Julian, I could barely see the ground at my feet.

I approached a steep spot where some large rocks jutted through the thin earth. Just then, Mateo bumped blindly into my leg, Julian leapt at the water bucket, and my foot slid sideways. Suddenly I was on my knees in the mud with water sloshing out of the overturned bucket. Pain rocketed through my leg where my shin made brutal contact with the rock.

Worse than the pain was the pitiful condition of my once-clean clothes. Mud! It covered my legs as well as my hands and arms, and when I brushed my hair from my eyes, it streaked my face as well. I sat in the mud, nursing the large bruise forming on my shin, and challenged the God who was remaking me thus. I was angry, and like Jonah outside Nineveh, I felt I had reason! The animals looked on sympathetically from a prudent distance.

Any illusions I may have harbored about an idyllic hermit life in the woods fled that hour. My options were starkly clear. Either I accepted living with mud, or I went back to the proverbial cleanliness of monastic life. I made my choice reluctantly as I picked up the empty bucket, trudged back down the hill, refilled it, and hung my sopping socks on the line to dry. If I had had Jonah's temerity, I might have imitated his attempt to run from God's call and boarded the next ship for Tarshish.

If this was the prophetic edge of religious life, I cursed

30

being chosen as a prophet. Prophets were called into nice, dry deserts, weren't they, not muddy valleys? What message could one bring back to the people of God covered with mud? I had to admit, however, that a mud-caked prophet would certainly be an affront to our sanitized culture. . . .

Like all times of initiation, my period on the muddy "mountaintop" eventually ended. I slid down from the heights of delusion literally on my backside and began a mud-stained career as a hermit with a determination to find the Lord amid all creation, even where it was lowliest and least lovely.

V

There Be Snakes

A THREATENING sky overhung Colt Run holler, breathing the damp chill of autumn. Haunted by a sense of urgency, I donned my grubbies and went out to survey the mess of wood rotting in the roofless cellar-hole beside my house. I needed to sort through the remnants and make room for a new supply of firewood, though I didn't yet know where that would come from.

Carefully descending the cement-block steps, I scanned the dirt-streaked floor nervously. The odor of wet earth, rotting logs, and mold greeted me. I sniffed, testing the air for the aroma of rotten cucumbers which, old-timers said, signaled the presence of copperheads. I'd been warned they were fond of wood-piles.

Slipping on a pair of heavy gloves, I began the scruffy job of shifting the old wood to make room for new logs and kindling, leaping wildly whenever I loosened a cascade of logs toward my vulnerable shins and feet.

To keep the wood off the floor, I had constructed a crude platform of two-by-sixes resting on pieces of available trash, including some old tires. The boards flipped up or swung sideways whenever I shifted their center of balance. I learned to tread lightly.

My worst apprehension about the platform, however, was what might lurk beneath it. I kept flicking glances toward my tennies and tried to keep even my toes from under the boards. After a while, I became absorbed in the task of shifting wet logs and sloughing off their old bark. The insects, worms, and thriving mold I uncovered discouraged me. It was a dreary task for a dreary day. However, my initial impression that the entire pile had rotted was dispelled when I rescued some remnants of viable firewood, and I was cheered to know that in the event of an early cold snap, I would be able to kindle a fire.

Picking up a piece of round wood from a heap in the corner, I suddenly froze in terror. Draped over the log directly before me was the ropey, diamond-patterned length of a copperhead. Judging by its double loop, it had to be near thirty inches long. I choked back a scream and stared at my worst fears realized. It lay still, apparently asleep and perhaps, I thought hopefully, dead. My hope was dashed by a ripple that ran the length of the sinewy body.

It hung only two feet from the side of the house. My gut instinct was to get the hell out of there and hope it would, too. But where would it go? Into some other protected spot in the woodpile where I might not see it before it saw me?

All the tales I'd heard about copperheads, those deadly scourges of the ridges, flashed through my brain. Still clutching the log, I took a cautious step backward. My unwanted guest did not move. Copperheads *did* have a harmless look-alike. Could this be one? I couldn't see whether it had an arrow-shaped head or whether its eye slits were vertical or horizontal. The tip of its tail was also out of sight, so I didn't know whether it was blunt or tapered. At that moment, however, my friend looked enough like a copperhead to satisfy any clinical interest I had in the species!

Time seemed oddly arrested. Instinct clamored for instant

34

action. Instead I stood immobilized, staring in fascinated horror. The copperhead also waited.

Gradually one thing impressed itself on me — the snake had to be killed, and I was the only one around to do it. The hazards of solitude! Quivering, I backed away and went for an axe lying near the front door. The oaken handle slipped in my sweaty palms. I secretly regarded this axe as an accident waiting to happen. In my hands, it could be more dangerous than a coiled copperhead.

With infinite caution, I retraced my steps toward the muddy brown snake. Yes, it was still there. Ideally I should sever its head in one fell swoop, but that head was out of sight among the logs. I didn't trust my courage or my aim sufficiently to stir up the dozing creature so it would lift its head to look at me.

My single option for a swift kill was to chop it in half. My stomach revolted at the prospect. As the seconds ticked away, another ripple through the draped body convinced me that it was about to slither away from my sight and the reach of my axe.

Bracing my feet, I raised the axe in both hands and swung it down, letting the weight of the axe head enhance the blow. Even so, my first stroke did not cut through the tough skin completely. The snake writhed, wounded but not dead. I struck again, and this time the front half of the snake flipped off the log toward my feet. I yelped and leapt. The back half twitched to the ground as blood and something yellowish oozed out. Hastily I turned, fighting nausea.

Deep breathing steadied me slightly. It had to be dead or would be soon. In the meantime, I needed some coffee. I retreated to the house, dropping the bloodied axe. Somehow, I hadn't realized that reptiles have red blood just like people. A dreadful loathing swept over me. For the first time in my life, I had consciously killed. And in most brutal fashion.

I sipped some coffee, letting its warmth gradually quell my

quivers. As I stared blankly amid a swirl of feelings, an image of the Mountain Woman insinuated itself in my mind. A tiny flicker of pride licked up inside me. I had just met and eliminated one of the most feared dangers in these hills, and I had done it, if not neatly, at least adequately. Something in me had changed.

It was a shock to discover that I could kill if I had to. It was also a shock to realize that I would not be magically protected against the perils infesting these hills to which the Lord had led me. Naiveté fell away like a cloak, and I felt dreadfully exposed. Anything could happen and might well do so. Divine Providence didn't include protection from the things I most feared.

But what I further began to recognize was that when danger had appeared, the strength to meet it had also been there. My resolution of the threat had not been particularly brave or brilliant, but neither had I run down the road screaming. I had not formulated contingency plans ahead of time, as a wiser person might have done, but perhaps it was better not to be always living in dread of the "what if's" in my life. Frightening things were bound to happen. But out of them unsuspected strengths might emerge.

By this time I was mildly hysterical. I began to giggle as I envisioned myself, the Mountain Mama, standing with raised axe before my cabin, daring any danger to approach. This was a significant switch from the fragile city girl, timidly peering out at a threatening wilderness.

Paradoxically, my heightened sense of vulnerability included a new sense of self-reliance. I did not need to be constantly protected by some great power in the sky; I had the ability to meet life's threats. A sense of personal power flooded me. If I were to become fully alive, I would meet with fear and panic, yes. Any venture into the unknown would lead me into dangers. The only question was this: Did my search for life include a consent to meet the snakes?

A tentative "Yes" began to form in my mind, and, with it, the scope of the possible in my life expanded. I had passed a pivotal point in my emerging call to a prophetic lifestyle. To have met a "snake in paradise" was not a sign that I shouldn't be living where such dangers lurked but rather proof that risks are inherent in any worthwhile venture.

My self-image shifted dramatically as I savored the empowerment I had experienced at the woodpile. I was now a tested "Mountain Woman," more confident and self-reliant. Other snakes have turned up since that grey day in early fall. But I know now that to find a snake from time to time in my Garden of Eden is to be expected . . . and that God, too, will be met in that moment.

VI

That First Christmas

A CHILL factor of 30 degrees below zero was predicted for the night. Already winds had dropped the thermometer reading to 5 degrees, and it was only four in the afternoon. Despite my almost continuous stoking, the wood stove was not doing a very effective job of keeping my house heated. Wearing thermal underwear and a heavy sweater, I kept warm by bustling about, preparing an Advent supper for Jeanne and Jane, who were coming over for our weekly get-together.

It was four days before my first Christmas in the holler, and West Virginia was in the grip of a record-breaking cold snap that had lasted nearly a week. The woodpile I had thought so huge in November had now dwindled so low that it would be completely gone by the day after Christmas.

Merciless nature threatened to invade my fragile shelter, and I wondered again if those who had shaken their heads at the foolhardiness of my new venture had been right. As the evening shadows fell, fear for survival crept into my soul. Only the sluggish fire kept killing cold at bay, a cold that seemed to penetrate through the very walls.

At dusk the sisters from down the road blew into my gloom, and I was cheered by their stories of survival through many years in these same circumstances. They gathered with me around the Advent wreath with its four blazing candles and sang the haunting "O Come, O Come, Emmanuel." My thoughts roamed to the many other households in these hills that Jeanne visited in her home nursing rounds. She had described poor families living in wretched shelters, huddled around wood fires or kerosene heaters as the cruel winds drove snow before them. O Emmanuel, when will you come to us?

"And ransom captive Israel." Ransom the captives of poverty and deprivation; ransom the captives of materialistic values; ransom a culture where the rich grow richer and the poor grow daily more desperate. Never before had I experienced what it was like to be living on the edge . . . nor realized that those who dwelt there daily were legion, even in this land of plenty.

To keep the pipes of my primitive water system from freezing, I had kept water dribbling slowly from the kitchen faucet. The well pump's constant racket was disturbing, however, so I temporarily turned off the faucet while we held our prayer service and ate supper.

Later, when I turned on the water to do dishes, a terrible hissing greeted me. Could the water have frozen in so short a time? My experienced friends sprang into action. While one identified the corner under the cupboard where the pipe sounded solid and began to wrap hot, wet towels around it, the other phoned a plumber.

We all cheered when, the ice miraculously loosened, water spurted from the spigot. But our joy was short-lived, for soon the gusher dribbled to a stop. Now the pump whined strangely. The friend on the phone said that a vulnerable point in the pump itself had probably frozen. At his direction, we aimed the hot air from a hair dryer at the narrow piping. To no avail. All I could do was turn off the pump before it burned itself out.

I had a small amount of water on hand, enough to do the dishes and to drink that night. The next morning, Jane and

Jeanne supplied me with several gallons of water from their house. The situation under the kitchen sink proved to be a disaster. The plastic pipes had splintered from the pressure of the ice, and a crack had appeared in the cast-iron pump head itself. There was no way this damage could be repaired before the New Year began because the icy hill was too treacherous for the plumber's truck to negotiate.

Friends from the parish offered me the shelter of their home during the holiday season. But, grateful though I was, I did not want to leave this little place that seemed so much like Bethlehem's stable. I was determined to remain as long as the electricity stayed on. A man from the church drove down with more gallons of water, some of it still hot, and a space heater.

On the morning of Christmas Eve, I tacked up some blankets to screen out the chill piercing through the windowed alcove and hung a large sheet of plastic across the front door as a shield against the drafts blowing in around its edges. I moved a chair as close to the stove as I dared. Then, wrapped in shawls and a stadium blanket, I sat down to contemplate the tiny crèche before me.

Without the whining of the water pump, the house was strangely quiet. Outside, the wind and snow muted all other sounds. "What am I doing here?" I asked. The answer seemed to reside in the scene on the little altar I had constructed. A young and poverty-stricken couple, forced to take shelter in a stable, were gazing in wonder at their newborn Child. I gazed with them. What else did I need?

I had food, water, shelter, and enough heat for the day. And here was this Poor Child, like so many millions of others, asking only for love, the one thing ultimately necessary. I had left my much-loved sisters in the monastery, partly because it was too sheltered, too secure, almost artificial in the kind of comfortable poverty that maintaining a large building with many people required. The Lady Poverty that I sought, delicate and elusive, seemed unattainable in a situation of corporate living.

Religious throughout this country wrestle with how to provide for the genuine needs of their members without getting trapped in our consumer-oriented culture. Security and provision for the future are preoccupations that seem reasonable, and even necessary. And yet, it is my impression that anxiety and worry often accompany the pursuit of security!

I had shared with my sisters their concerns about balancing poverty and security when I was a part of the administration in my own religious community. At the same time, I had contemplated the picture of Francis and Clare, freely tossing all their cares on the Lord and discovering — joyously — how little they really needed besides the experience of that surpassing Love.

I remembered the appealing story of another Christmas Eve in 1223, when St. Francis led the poor villagers of Greccio caroling up a hillside to a simple Christmas scene. A live ox and donkey stood tethered to a manger in a cave snugged into the hillside. There, in the womb of the earth, Christmas mass was celebrated, and Francis conveyed his endless delight that we mortals are so loved that the God of all creation had been born a child among us. As Thomas of Celano, his biographer, wrote, "The vision of the Child Jesus . . . had been forgotten in the hearts of many; but, by the working of [God's] grace, it was brought to life again through [Francis]."

Something of those peasants' experience gripped me as I focused on the Child amid the chill of my Appalachian dwelling. A warmth filled me that had little to do with firewood. It had a great deal to do with discovering the One Thing Necessary for me to live my personal Poor Clare vocation with the utmost integrity.

"Few things are necessary, indeed, only one," Jesus had said to the harried Martha. I knew deep in my soul — indeed, had always known — that only One Thing would ever satisfy me: total transformation in the image of my God. And here was my God choosing poverty and powerlessness. In the cold and quiet, I made a conscious choice to live in need and unfulfillment. With that choice, I entered a new stage of my Franciscan calling. And in the distance, I seemed to hear the bells of Christmas ringing out for me.

Thanks to Jane and Jeanne's trusty red truck, we were able to get out of the holler to attend Midnight Mass. The ridges were ghostly white under the stars as we drove through the still night to the parish church. We had picked up old Jack from along Colt Ridge to be our guest at the services, which included a joyous sing-along accompanied by dulcimer and fiddle. Jack happily tapped his foot in time with the familiar carols.

But during the mysterious celebrations that followed, he asked in loud stage whispers, "What's that thing the minister's got on? What's in that gold cup? Is that wine?" and his old Baptist soul shivered. The only part of the Mass that Jack seemed to really understand was the Kiss of Peace — at least, he most heartily participated in this warm exchange of holiday greetings.

Afterward, I returned to my own little Bethlehem, my house of peace. As the stars began to fade that first Christmas morning, I reflected that this was the most wonderful Christmas of my life, surpassing even those magical ones of early childhood. A few pine branches stuck in a bucket constituted my "tree," and holly from shrubs near the broken-down barn graced my kitchen table.

As I waited for the wood stove to blaze up, Merton crawled, purring, onto my lap. In the flickering candlelight, the rough walls of the hermitage glowed warmly, surrounding and sheltering me as did the arms of God. "Joy to the world. The Lord is come!"

"Little House in a Holler"

VII

Be It Ever So Brown

A S I turned into the entrance of my drive, my breath quickened and my sweaty palms gripped the steering wheel more firmly. I needed to maintain momentum in order to crest the rise ahead of me. Rocky outcroppings on my left nudged my vehicle toward the ten-foot drop into the run on my right. When I felt the tires begin an inexorable slide sideways, I shifted into four-wheel drive. Would the bald tires find enough traction in the slick mud, or would my nightmare of pitching into the creek be realized this time?

I fought with the wheel, cautiously applied more gas, and once more topped the rise, then began a slippery descent into puddles six inches deep. Slithering and sloshing, I made my way up the drive to the house. For once I would not have to backpack my groceries from the road to the front door.

My first autumn and winter in Colt Run proved to be a rugged initiation. A long fall yielded to a winter of record-breaking snow and cold. The "yard" around the house was a morass of mud with a few clumps of bunch grass in the ruts. Nothing is more dreary than mud in November — except mud in February. I enjoyed an abundance of both and swore that before next fall, grass would be covering this brown expanse that stretched to my front steps.

Once it turned cold enough to freeze, the oozy mud became solid ridges over which I daily tripped as I brought in my quota of logs from the woodpile, which I had unwisely situated *up* the hillside from the front door. When the sun came out, the mud became slush that sucked at my feet and splashed over the top of my knee-high boots.

Mud taunted and challenged me every time I had to trek up the hillside to the outhouse. It greeted me unfailingly on my way to the compost heap behind the shed. Mud clogged the wheels of my Radio Flyer wagon that I had to coax up the long drive and down the road to Jeanne and Jane's so that I could fill milk jugs with water from their outside spigot. (I had unhappily discovered that the old well at my house was badly polluted.)

As I tugged and struggled with my wagon, I was reminded of the mud-clogged chariot wheels of the Egyptians, bogged down in the Red Sea. I took to reminding God that I was *not* the enemy. Did everything have to be so difficult?

On Sunday mornings I had to trek out to the road to be picked up because the soft muck of my long drive was usually impassable for vehicles. I carried my shoes in a backpack and changed out of my muddy boots once we reached the church. In spring, the perennial puddles abounded with tadpoles. Fascinating as these were, it was small comfort that my drive was a wetland nursery.

Throughout that first long winter, mud invaded my house because I didn't even have a stoop where I could remove my boots before stepping over the threshold. With rag and broom and sweeper, I warred with the encroaching mud. It never went away. It simply moved from boot to rag to hands to sink. . . .

And it began to intrude into my soul. Anger gave way to depression. Did life have to be such an unending and hopeless struggle? The insecurity of my situation bore down on me as I stared out at the brown ridges surrounding my house. My life

46

seemed to have no sense or reason. The words of Jeremiah, tossed into a miry pit by his enemies, came to me:

> The waters flowed over my head,
>   and I said, "I am lost!"
> I called upon your name, O Lord,
>   from the bottom of the pit;
> You heard me call, "Let not your ear
>   be deaf to my cry for help!"
> You came to my aid when I called to you;
>   you said, "Have no fear!" (Lam. 3:54-57)

Wryly I noted that the prophet had been encouraged to have no fear but that God had left him in that miry pit.

I began to hate the color brown. By February it surrounded me on all sides. The fields were a dreary shade as weeds wearily collapsed from repeated beatings by snow and rain. Dead brown leaves lay in flattened heaps on the rocky hillsides. Even the clouds seemed dun-colored.

February stretched ahead endlessly, a brown, dismal month brimming with the dregs of winter without a hint of spring. For me it was the longest month of the year. The daily round of stoking the wood fire, cleaning the ashes out of the stove, praying, and sewing lost all its earlier charm. I *existed* from one day to the next. I wanted to run from what I began to call The Brown Experience.

But I knew I had to face this greatest challenge to solitary life head-on. Ennui, boredom, is known to be the "noonday devil" of hermits. The great temptation is to find some escape from this experience. I sensed that I was being called to enter fully into the depths of this dread brownness — go through it, sink my roots deep into it — and to believe that doing so would enable me to come out on the other side of this bleak period more alive than ever before.

47

So I deliberately studied the depressing landscape and consciously felt all the uncomfortable feelings of sadness, depression, and death that it evoked and graphically symbolized. I even wrote poems about the mud. I did not attempt to find any special goodness in this experience but merely strove for peaceful co-existence with the doldrums of a season in which nothing seemed to end, nothing to begin.

With inexorable slowness, day flowed into day. Eventually February merged with March, and spring began its shy approach. With it came a wonder. The mud began to bloom! Small green things appeared amid the ruts, and sparse grass began to spread. A blush of greenery suffused the steep ridge outside my kitchen window. One day I caught a glimpse of yellow as I was wringing out laundry and rushed outdoors to ascertain whether my eyes were telling me true.

Yes! A clump of daffodils was struggling to emerge through the tangled brown of last year's brambles. I knelt beside it, heedless of the mud, and cupped a golden bloom in my hands. Fresh and pure, it glowed back at me. Fragrance filled my nostrils. The first winter was ending.

A familiar voice whispered softly, "Take note. In the midst of mud, flowers will bloom by your boots."

VIII

Mighty White Hunter

I N THE pre-dawn darkness, something disturbs my sleep. Soft footsteps on the circular stairs to my loft bedroom alert me. I can hear them coming across the carpeting, and suddenly there is a jolt as something hits the bed. Cautiously I pull my arm from under the covers and encounter a fur bundle that begins to purr.

Merton, my white tom, is intent on awakening the provider of breakfast. If I don't rise up at once, disturbing noises reach my ears. A plastic statue clatters from a windowsill; pencils and papers on the desk rattle. Finally I am subject to direct molestation when Merton walks up my chest and gently, yes, ever so softly, pats my face.

By this time, I'm grinning in the dark, and when I slit my eyes open, I see a small, pointy face with luminous dark eyes peering down at me expectantly. His Highness is hungry, and it's time I did something about it.

So begins another day at Beth Shalom hermitage, where I dwell with Tom Merton, the Mighty White Hunter. How much better to be wakened thus than by some heartless alarm! I don't understand how Merton knows it is 5:30 A.M., but he's as punctual as any clock radio and definitely more personal.

Merton tumbles down the steps ahead of me and lashes his tail impatiently as I splash cold water on my face. Only after he's crouched, crunching his Friskies in the corner, am I free to start a fire in the wood stove and make a cup of coffee.

As I settle down for some moments of quiet meditation, the inevitable happens — His Highness is ready to go outside, and the following conversation ensues:

Merton, nose pointing at the front door: "M-m-yout."
Me: "No."
Merton: "M-yout!"
Me: "No."
Merton: "Mrr-yout NOW!"
Me: "No, too dark."
Merton, while scratching at the door: "Mrrr, mrrr. . . ."
Me: "Don't try that."
Merton: Scratch, scrabble, scratch, scratch. . . .
Me: "STOP THAT!"
Merton: "W-out!"
Me: "Oh, all right."

Five minutes later . . .

Merton, from outside: "Mm-you!"
Me: "Too soon."
Merton: "Mm-you-in."
Me: "No, not yet."
Merton: "Min, min, min!"
Me: "You really want in?"
Merton: "M-nyea."
Me: "Okay, but stay in, will you?"
Merton: "M-mnn."

I'm slowly learning Cat, a language that is rather simple but capable of extraordinary nuances of feeling. The greatest difficulty I have with the language is the major part played by the tail. But Merton is training me with infinite patience despite my obvious limitations.

Distraction or delight, Merton took over my life that day in June I brought him home, a tiny white ball of fluff that could sit in the palm of my hand. The only white kitten among his litter mates, he appealed to me because of the dignity he displayed even in the rough-and-tumble games of kittenhood. Even then he was a prince.

I wanted a cat primarily as a companion, only secondarily as a mouser. My new friend would reveal special talents in both arenas. Given his bearing, I suspected — rightly — that there would be some contest of wills in the offing, and I was determined to keep the upper hand. Little did I know . . .

The very first night, I introduced Merton to the lined box I'd prepared for him, which I had set next to my bed. I then blew out the Coleman lantern and got under the covers. A piteous cry from somewhere down on the floor wavered up through the darkness. I suddenly remembered that this little guy had never slept alone before, apart from the warm bodies of brothers and sisters and mother. What could I do? I reached down and plucked him from the box.

I was rewarded with a purr of satisfaction. That purring prowled around the bed, across the pillow above my head and on down past my feet, as this budding royalty inspected his domain. He finally settled down, a tiny weight on my tummy, wrapped his tail over his nose, and fell contentedly asleep.

The next morning I awoke with a sinking feeling that a precedent had been set which would be hard to reverse. I was right. To this day, I share my bed with my prince. It took Merton only a few weeks to train me into an obedient human being who knew when to let him in and out, what food he liked, and when to serve it — frequently!

I had thought I knew what to expect living with a cat. After all, I had grown up with cats. What I hadn't been prepared for was the storm of emotions this kitten precipitated in my heart. Suddenly I had someone to care for, someone who needed me, someone to come home to. The solitude of my hermitage was taken over by a lovable presence that laid claims on me I could not ignore.

I had not known I was lonely for love until Merton began to fill up some of the empty space in my heart. The first hint of my entanglement was how anxious I became whenever this curious kitten was out of my sight. Beyond the hermitage door was a wild world of hazards. I worried about my neighbors' cat; about the occasional vehicle on the road; about traps or trees too tall; about how easily a small cat could get lost in the great big woods.

I began to find it difficult to settle into prayer when my little friend was out wandering, and I would listen, alert for the mew announcing his presence on the front steps. I did not welcome this kind of worry and tried to convince myself that cats are independent and self-reliant creatures. Although this was certainly true of Merton, it did not ease the little burden of anxiety I carried, the little burden of loving and needing the loved one.

Merton had come to me with an incipient case of distemper. When his golden eyes turned runny and he became alarmingly lethargic, I knew I had to get him to a vet immediately. This involved a forty-five-minute drive on a hot summer day with a potentially wild cat rocketing around my Bronco.

I made small holes in a box, put my kitten inside, and tied the lid shut. Five minutes into the drive, a frantic white fury had clawed its way free of the box, emitting distressed shrieks, while I tried to concentrate on negotiating the rutted road leading to the highway.

Pulling over, I closed all the windows tightly, haunted by a picture of my panicked kitten leaping out onto the busy road to be killed or lost forever. I tried to soothe him with words, but nothing quieted the frantic, squealing bundle of fur that tore around inside my vehicle.

I prayed desperately that the needle-like claws of the careening kitten wouldn't rake me in passing and cause me to swerve off the road. More than once, I had to grope blindly under my feet to pull a terrified cat out from between gas pedal and brake. For brief moments, Merton would cling to my shoulder, claws piercing to my collarbone. People must have wondered about this two-headed driver they passed on the road.

I was a basket case by the time we arrived at the vet's. What made things worse was my discovery that the office wouldn't be open for another hour — an hour neither Merton nor I could spend sweltering in the closed Bronco under the summer sun. I spied a MacDonald's nearby and used the drive-through service, ordering a hamburg for myself and ice water for a panting Merton. The service people must have been curious about why I barely cracked the window open to give my order and seemed to have only one hand when accepting it — my other hand was firmly gripping the squirming creature on the seat. We parked under a shady tree and waited.

When I finally left the vet with medicine and a certified pet carrier cooping up a still-protesting Merton, I breathed easier. I needed some groceries, so I stopped at the local IGA. It seemed safe to leave the windows slightly open so that Merton, still alternately growling and mewling, wouldn't suffer heat prostration while I made a brief foray into the store.

I returned within ten minutes to find a hole chewed through the carrier and my precious mite nowhere in sight. Frantically, I searched the large parking lot and scanned the highway, fearing to spot a flattened bit of fur wherever I turned.

The heavy ache in my chest and the tears smarting my eyes proved the inroads this creature had made in my heart during the mere ten days we had lived together. Desperately, I paced the lot, crying "Here, kitty, kitty!" in that silly, high-pitched voice that humans use with cats.

Could he have headed for the green grass of neighboring houses? Or dived down into the gully beside the parking lot? Perhaps if I ran a "lost" ad in the local paper and put a message on the radio, someone would let me know if they found him alive? My despair mounted with each passing minute as I contemplated the numberless hazards a busy parking lot in the middle of town posed for a kitten.

I was still wandering hopelessly among the cars when I caught a glimpse of something white on the walk in front of the store. Was it? Could it be? I ran recklessly across the parking lot. There, sure enough, trotting among the feet of passersby, was Merton. Then, as now, he paid no heed to my calls. Smiling apologetically at curious people, I swooped down upon my errant kitten, relief flooding me as my hands closed about the furry little body.

From that day forward, I harbored no illusions about who had the power in my household — nor did Merton. As he grew, the secret history of his breeding became evident. His angora genes were obvious as he developed into a gorgeous, snow-white creature with a double coat of fine, long hair covering a soft and fluffy undercoat. His somewhat pointy face with its slightly tilted nose was topped off with pinkish triangles that perked at every sound.

His fathomless amber eyes projected an intelligence that was intimidating — a wisdom predating humanity. His gaze was serene, commanding, and impish by turns. Mere words were unnecessary when those expressive eyes fixed on you. You *knew* you were expected to do something, and at once!

But even more eloquent than those mysterious eyes was Merton's long, plumy tail, which signaled every emotion, every nuance of response to his environment. He could be stretched out on the living room rug, apparently oblivious to his surroundings, but the tip of that sinuous tail would be twitching. My placid white tom was about to become a white streak.

Cat fanciers have noted that when a feline tail is upright, it signals an alert and happy interest. So when I would spy Merton at the far end of the drive and call him, I would watch to see what that fluffy thirteen inches behind him would do. If it stood up, even if Merton had spared me no glance, I would know he had heard me and had some intention of responding. But if that tail remained horizontal, the Mighty Hunter was not about to be disturbed.

Curling, lashing, drooping, or waving, this fluffy appendage was an accurate indicator of my little brother's feelings and desires. It proclaimed him crown prince of the realm, handsome and graceful, occasionally condescending, but just as often playful. Merton could concentrate as totally on a piece of crinkly tin foil as he could on his breakfast.

Whether ensconced on the couch or streaking across the field in furious pursuit, Merton was simply elegant. "How does he stay so white?" was an invariable question of guests who had recently trekked up the muddy drive. I had no answer — it was another of Merton's enduring mysteries. All I knew was that he worked at it with total absorption whenever he came in from hunting forays.

Merton was indeed a Mighty White Hunter and frequently brought home prizes from the chase. Unfortunately for me, hunting was strictly an outdoor sport for him, not to be engaged in within the house. Mice outside were prey; mice inside were playmates.

Occasionally I clashed with Merton over the victims of his hunt and would intervene if a bunny or chipmunk seemed lively enough to make good an escape once I pried it from between Merton's clamped jaws. But my efforts at Franciscan peacemaking were not appreciated.

I had to accept Merton as the hunter he was, with his

quirks and instincts. Thanks to him, I began to learn that loving demanded acceptance of others' views and ideas, even when these differed from mine. I also learned that loving meant becoming defenseless against pain, heartache, and tears; that, inevitably, giving my heart to another meant taking the risk of having it rejected or even broken.

Merton padded into my heart and created a hole that no one but he could fill. My many years in a cloister had taught me to guard my heart against "too much attachment to things of this world." I was not encouraged to give or receive overt forms of affection. It was a lesson I found difficult to unlearn. But a certain white cat burrowed under my fence and took up residence, ignoring that it was "posted" territory.

Letting myself love, becoming vulnerable to worry, fear of loss, and need for the loved one . . . in a word, becoming defenseless in the soft paws of a purring cat began to pry my heart open to loving others in my life with more genuine affection. In particular, I began to appreciate the value of physical contact.

Cats are literally touching animals. They brush up against your legs, purr wildly when stroked, and generally relish a warm lap to curl up in. Merton was no exception — even though he retained the right to determine when and how he would take his strokes. I loved his soft, silky fur and found, when I had to be away for a couple of days, that I missed our petting times, possibly more than he did.

Being entrusted with someone to love and being loved in return has literally recreated me. An abiding loneliness has been erased, not just because a cat lives with me but because through accepting the vulnerability of loving, I have found the whole world a friendlier place. Loving has freed me from a neediness that made me hold onto all I could. Love has taught me a poverty of heart that counts wealth in the happiness of another.

Loving a little animal was a safe beginning for me. Rejec-

56

tion was not likely if food and fondling were provided in adequate measure. It was a good place for me to start removing the brick wall that years of fear and distrust had erected. Despite his natural cat-like aloofness, Merton gave me far more than I could give him just by his trusting presence in my house.

He had no inhibitions about making his needs known and would follow me from room to room, nudge me, trip me, or crawl up the leg of my jeans if I did not respond. I learned that getting things done wasn't very important compared with brushing Merton's coat or petting him or just sitting when he suddenly demanded a lap.

Perhaps even more importantly, I learned that love meant letting the beloved go freely where he will. Each morning, I must open the front door and let Merton out to do his cat-things. Danger to my little brother (as exists in the wilderness of the holler) is danger to me, because my happiness and well-being have become inextricably enmeshed with those of a vulnerable little hunter who roams the hills as if he owns them. Yet I must grant Merton this freedom to come and go, to be himself — the Mighty White Hunter of butterflies and bunnies and birds, as well as the accidental mouse. I recognize that I was the first victim of this fearless hunter, and I have no regrets.

IX

Beware the Wild Roses

I AM rudely grabbed from behind, and something sharp pierces my heavy sweater. I try a dip-and-turn maneuver in an attempt to disengage from the fierce grasp, but the briar rose merely hooks more wicked thorns into my back, threatening to rake my skin if I make any unwise move. By now, as my second winter in the holler draws to a close, I have developed a healthy respect for wild roses — coupled with a fierce desire to root them out.

A slight breeze, and another branch waves toward me, snaring my hair and flickering dangerously close to my right eye. I'd already surrendered my knit cap when overhanging thorns had snatched it off my head. That snagged ruin, now stuffed in my jeans' pocket, bears eloquent testimony to the curving thorns, marshalled two by two along the ten-foot branches of the rose-bushes dominating the banks of the run in my front field.

My long-handled pruners and shrub clippers are proving totally inadequate for the job at hand. True, I can cut a branch off a towering clump of briars, but even though I'm wearing leather gloves, pulling it free from the entangled growth is all but impossible. The rosebush fiercely guards its own, dead or alive. In fact, my attempts to cut it down merely prune it, encouraging more prolific growth.

Stooping low, I attempt to crawl free of the bush's vicious hold. I carefully loosen the thorns scraping my scalp and break the branch hooked in my sweater. I emerge, scratched and bleeding, from yet one more round with the bane of the hills, Rosa multiflora. The victor waves arching branches in the spring breeze, and I back off a prudent distance. Multiflora can reach out to snag any warm-blooded creature within five feet.

When I first moved to Colt Run and discovered the delicate blossoms of the wild rose, I was entranced. Here was a wild flower worthy indeed of preservation. When I mentioned this to my neighbor, all I got was a pitying glance and the remark that wild roses have caused more grief to farmers and herders than poison ivy. A few months of frustrated attempts to tame the teeming jungle about my new home proved how right she was!

Everywhere the stubborn briars were taking over, and other, more benign plants were being crowded out. One deeply rooted clump of multiflora blocked the path around my house. The former tenants had attempted to trim it back and instead had cultivated luxuriant new growth of thorny shoots.

I took my problem to the local Southern States Co-op that served the farmers of the area.

"How do you kill wild rosebushes?"

"Multiflora? Now there's a very tough question. Nothing normally can kill them."

"Not even Japanese beetles?" I asked, recalling the havoc these pests wreak on garden roses.

"Nope. There aren't enough beetles to make a dent in multiflora. Getting rid of those briars is tough and dangerous work."

From a shelf, I picked up a preparation that was advertised as a brush and shrub killer. "Will this work on multiflora?"

A wary look crossed the face of the friendly man behind the counter. "Well, it claims to," he allowed, "but you have to be careful how you use it."

I studied the label and noted that it mandated a back-carried spray outfit and protective clothing as well as a mask and gloves. "Pretty powerful stuff?"

"It is. And the runoff from it is deadly, likely to contaminate creeks or springs. It only works if it's sprayed on when the leaves are coming out. It acts like a cancer — makes cells multiply so fast that the plant eventually exhausts itself and dies."

"Eventually?"

"Well, for the first few weeks, the plant grows wild, just like it was fertilized. But after a while, it withers up."

"Then you have to cut it down and drag it off to be burned?"

"Yep. The spray doesn't really kill the roots, though, so you should dig them out, too."

As if all that work weren't cost enough, the price of sufficient chemical to kill just one full-sized multiflora clump far exceeded what I could afford to spend on weeds.

An older man who had listened with interest to this discussion at the counter chimed in, "I don't like those kinds of chemicals. They're expensive and dangerous. Me, I've found something that works just as well and only costs a fraction of that. It's the 14 percent ammonium nitrate they sell in bulk for fertilizing. It makes them roses grow like crazy until they just die. I've been killing them off on a hillside that I'm making into a garden spot."

"Ammonium nitrate. What do you think of it?" I asked the proprietor.

"Well, I've never heard of using it for that. Who knows, it might work," he said dubiously.

Another helpful soul joined the debate. "I don't like using any of that kind of stuff. It's bad for the land and bad for the

61

water. Now, I've been looking after the orchard at the place where my mother used to live, and it was nearly choked out with rose briars. But I took care of them, and so far, they haven't come back."

"Oh?"

"Yes. First of all, I took my tractor-mower and cut the bushes down as close to the ground as I could. After they withered up some, I raked them off to be burned and dug out the roots as deep as I could go with a pick and shovel. What I couldn't get — and there's no way you can dig deep enough to get all the roots — I packed with rock salt, which I covered with a good layer of dirt. That's so the deer wouldn't get at it and lick it all away. I think that salt just burned out the rest of the roots. Leastwise, they haven't shown up again. And runoff from the salt isn't as harmful as these chemical herbicides they sell."

"Well, I need to think about this," I murmured as I left the store, more discouraged than when I'd come in. It was clear that only heavy machines and major investment could deal adequately with multiflora. Later I talked with a backhoe operator who had found that even bulldozers didn't protect a person from the raking thorns of wild roses. He said he'd rolled his dozer over a bush, crushing it under the treads, only to have it rise up behind him and fall over his head, nearly putting out his eyes. I could believe it!

Back home, I surveyed the clusters of briars between my drive and the run. Other clumps dotted the bank sloping down from the woods. They mingled with more welcome briars of raspberry and blackberry. The entangled mess reminded me of lines from T. S. Eliot about the hopeless struggle to find words to express adequately one's truth and feelings:

And so each venture
Is a new beginning, a raid on the inarticulate

With shabby equipment always deteriorating
In the general mess of imprecision of feeling,
Undisciplined squads of emotion.
And what there is to conquer
By strength and submission. . . .

The general mess . . . inadequate means . . . undisciplined squads of emotion. . . . So it truly was! My intense anxiety over the wild rosebushes mirrored my discomfort with an anger that was rooted in my heart, an anger that I was reluctant to admit. Denial of this powerful emotion resulted in suppression of almost all my passions — an exhausting business. Feelings of fatigue and inadequacy frequently paralyzed me.

There was no quick fix, no magic bullet with which to slay these undisciplined squads marauding within me. My first step had to be recognition and acceptance of these forces so deeply rooted in my psyche. It was a humbling moment when I finally looked honestly at what so frequently choked my energies or cast gloom over my best endeavors. Anger, rooted in resentment and guilt as well as fear and anxiety, gnawed relentlessly at the ragged edges of my peace.

I resented how difficult the simplest things often were in this primitive setting. I felt guilty about leaving the monastery where I had lived for so many years. I was full of fear about the future, as well as anxiety about the present. All these emotions made me angry. My feelings were not particularly rational, but there they were — in their general mess of imprecision.

When I began to put them into words, risked naming and defining what caused them, I was astounded to discover that they weren't the towering enemies of my peace that I had imagined them to be. In fact, they proved to be valuable indicators of growth and provided me with power and strength to deal with the realities of my solitary life.

At first I only dared to make small forays into this uncomfortable world of negative feelings. As with my assault on the wild roses, my best hope seemed to be in getting at the smaller briars before they became too entangled. This meant a self-awareness and an honesty I was not used to. My daily journaling proved to be the arena where I dared to notice and acknowledge the proliferating briars in my inner world.

One day I risked exploring why I felt guilty about leaving the cloister where I had lived for over thirty years. I realized that it wasn't having left the *place* that bothered me but concern that I had let down the sisters with whose lives my life had been intermingled. Carefully I examined this notion. Could my continued presence in the monastery really have benefited the group?

My physical strength had not tolerated the normal stresses of community living very well. I had developed a chronic muscle problem that frequently sidelined me from daily activities. As I considered things objectively, it appeared that this physical weakness was among the signs from God indicating that I venture a more solitary life. My sisters in the monastery had seen this even more clearly than I when I had made my original discernment. And I knew they had genuinely rejoiced with me as I recovered health and vigor in the country setting of my hermitage.

The guilt I felt diminished as I dared to write about it in my journal. And with it, some anger. A new peace began to grow.

Suddenly it is my second spring. One morning in mid-May, I throw open my window, and a breathtaking fragrance wafts through. I thrill as I step out onto the dew-wet grass and behold cascades of white blossoms adorning all the pesky briars I have been unable to eradicate. Softly the spring breeze brushes my cheek, urging me to make my peace with forces that are beyond my control, forces that are both dark and beautiful.

At this moment I begin to feel differently about the challenge of beating back the jungle. Not everything wild and unruly needs to be uprooted, I realize. Without multiflora, spring in Appalachia would be appreciably different, appreciably less lovely. The clusters of white roses cascading down the towering bushes add vitality and grace to the greening hillsides.

Perhaps anger has its place in my inner world, too? Surely it has provided me with valuable surges of energy so that I have accomplished feats I once thought impossible. Would I have ever accomplished the move to Colt Run holler had I not been empowered by my anger over the numberless obstacles blocking my way?

Outside my window, hummingbirds zip about, sharing the sweet nectar of the wild roses with bees and droning wasps. During the past winter, the tenacious roots and tangled shoots of the briars prevented precious bits of soil from eroding off the stony slopes of the ridges. Now they provide shelter for rabbits, moles, and other hunted things.

Multiflora and its exuberant associates have something to teach me. I sit on the wooden porch steps and survey the lush scene, pruners and clippers forgotten. Quietly I reconsider my mindless attack on the interlocking system of life around and within me. Multiflora, like anger, has its necessary place in an ecosystem that demands both stubbornness and vitality.

In the silence, birdsongs echo from all directions. I watch goldfinches perch on thistles, and an indigo bunting alight on a swaying frond of wild oats. Among the grasses (growing so much faster than I can mow or weed-whip into submission), multitudes of white, pink, and yellow flowers bloomed. Creepers and crawlers wind their busy ways among them.

This is the world the Lord has given me, vibrant with unquenchable vigor as spring returns, thanks in part to the stubborn, thorny multiflora that has held the land in place through freeze and deluge.

Instead of cutting and hacking, perhaps I should be praying and listening. The wind whispers something, and the young rose leaves waggle with delight. The sun warms the pines, teasing out their rich fragrance to blend with the delicate perfume of rosebuds. I breathe deeply and grow still.

Beware what wild roses can do to you! You may be seduced into cherishing what you once planned to destroy.

X

Windows of the World

I GNAWED thoughtfully on the end of the ballpoint as I struggled to find words for the mix of emotions stirring deep within me. For the past two months, I, along with the rest of the world, had lived with attention focused on a tiny country in the Persian Gulf. Tonight the radio had announced that bombs had ceased to fall on that hapless land. What did that mean to me?

I noticed that a full moon was rising over the eastern ridge behind my house, spilling silvery light down the dark slopes. It was so quiet . . . no longer did I hear deadly explosions in the background or a guided missile screaming overhead. Slowly I began to write:

> As evening thickens,
>   the candle glows brighter.
> A great quiet descends
>   where bombs fell only last night. . . .

Had bombs been falling in Colt Run holler? Indeed they had, for I knew in the deepest fiber of my being that bombs falling on any part of the world were also falling on me. The Persian Gulf conflict had been but one more vivid reminder of the truth which a contemplative experiences with keen awareness — that the human family is but one body. What harms any member harms the whole.

The longer I dwell in solitude, the more united I feel with others. I don't see the faces of starving Somalians; the devastations of hurricanes, floods, and war; the horror of riots and beatings. I hear of these and other catastrophes only on the daily radio news. But that is sufficient. To know of these events is a call to bear the burdens of others in my heart and carry them to the Heart of all Love, from whence alone, I know, healing can come.

Not all my human contacts are so distant. Phone calls and letters bring me into more direct relationship with an amazing variety of people. Some are cherished friends I've known since preschool days; others are total strangers who contact me because they have read something I have written. There is a man in prison in Ohio with whom I'd attended grade school and a woman inmate in a correctional institution in the East who shares my passion for cats.

I receive airmail letters from Holland, India, and Africa, and phone calls from California and Texas. "How does this fit with being a hermit?" I sometimes muse during my hours of prayer. It *does* fit, I intuitively know, for my life is not meant to be lived for myself alone, however isolated I might be physically. Perhaps I am to live surrounded by silence so that I might more clearly discern the cries of others? Perhaps there need to be listening hearts in our noisy world, persons whose contribution to peace and tranquility — yes, possibly to sanity itself — is simply to hear and to care?

Whatever answer I may eventually come to, it seems clear to me that God expects me to foster and maintain a surprising number of relationships. Every year I scrimp and save in order to have sufficient postage to send my annual Christmas letter to friends, relatives, and benefactors. And every year the number of cards I have to answer grows larger.

Before December 25th dawns, the cupboard doors in my kitchen are bright with cheery cards, a humbling testament to the many who remember me with love during the holiday season. I ponder over this amazing display as I sip my luncheon soup one day during Advent, noting the handmade card from another hermit-friend; the rice-paper greeting with pressed flowers from Bethlehem; the carefully printed note from a child.

"Wealth beyond all measure," I reflect, feeling teary-eyed over this tangible display of love and friendship. Christmas evokes a more vivid demonstration of a marvel that continues year-round. Sometimes I sigh over the numbers of unanswered letters by my typewriter, but I am grateful for each one nonetheless.

Should a hermit have a telephone? Those who ask such a question probably envision a witchy, people-hating recluse who keeps a loaded shotgun at the ready to discourage visitors or who flees into the woods at their approach. I sincerely hope I am neither. A phone is a necessity of daily life, as I see it, although I am careful about how frequently I use it. I welcome most calls . . . except from those ubiquitous telemarketers who always call just at the least convenient moment!

I seldom invite visitors to my home. I love my solitary days and nights. But for certain people, I make exceptions. Among these are sisters from the monastery in Ohio who are seeking some time of peaceful solitude. Once each summer they come as a group to picnic in the cool shade of my pines and walk the country road past the pond and the pastures further down the holler. More frequently they come singly for weeklong retreats or days of personal recollection. On occasion, I will receive a late-night call and offer my guest bed to a woman who needs refuge from a difficult domestic situation.

Except for Sisters Jeanne and Jane, I know most of my neighbors only by face and name — these friendly folk with whom I exchange a wave in passing. Jeanne and Jane have made frequent hospitality a part of their lifestyle and have built a couple of guest hermitages near their cabin. I will occasionally act as spiritual director for one of their retreatants.

Jeanne, Jane, and I meet weekly for an evening of prayer and sharing. Through them, I learn much about the life of the people in this struggling section of Appalachia. Jeanne's rounds as a home-health nurse take her into some of the farthest reaches of the county, and she regales us with stories of the picturesque folks she encounters. She also relates with un-denied anger the desperate situations of poverty and depriva-tion she too frequently discovers in her travels.

Through Jeanne, I have developed a sense of community with my unseen neighbors, those who live unmentioned on the margins of society. My choice to be a hermit places me physically among them, and I feel my obligation to be a "sister" to all of them through prayer. For them and with them I pray, and share the vicissitudes of poverty and the love that holds them to this harsh and beautiful land.

Appalachia is an old land, an area of mountains eroding and now sinking back into the earth. Once higher than the Rockies, these rounded, tree-frosted heights are cloaked in a wisdom so ancient that it clashes with the raw newness of the Great Discoveries of modern technology. I intuitively sense the enduring knowledge of these mute hills, hills that existed long before civilization evolved.

My moment among these ridges will be brief, however long I stay. But I might be favored with a glimpse through windows that are almost eternal of the world which truly lasts, of rela-tionships that bind body and spirit to this earth of which we are all born. And . . .

Perhaps an ancient seed of strange,
    forgotten bloom

70

may rise to blossom
    this very spring,
nourished in the mold of deaths long past,
and now rebirthed
    in the ever-living, ever-waiting earth.

All my relationships, near and far, are part of this fostering of a new hope of communion among all peoples. As a hermit, I seek solitude, not so much to be alone as to bring together in myself all the disparate strands of life in our world.

It is not a work I can do; only the Spirit can accomplish this reweaving into unity. I am privileged to be part of the loom.

"Deer Who Appear"

XI

Deer Who Appear

ARRESTED in mid-step in my descent from the loft, I stare intently through the back window. Shyly a doe emerges from the trees. Two fawns leap from behind her, springing playfully about on stilted legs. I hardly dare to breathe as the graceful mother anxiously scans the field for danger. Satisfied, she begins to graze while her twins sniff flowers or butt at each other.

I shift my position to keep them in view, and the doe catches a hint of movement. She throws up her head with a snort of alarm that freezes the fawns into near invisibility. With a swift turn, she herds her offspring out of sight into the comparative safety of the wooded ridge.

Sighing lightly, I continue my way down the steps and toward my prayer space. For more than two years I have waited for the graced moment when these shy creatures of the wild would appear within view of my windows.

Waiting . . . a watchword of my life in solitude. What a toll it demands of my meager store of patience! How frequently I grow depressed when the glowing visions that had enticed me toward hermit life refuse to materialize out of the brushy growth of my inner landscape.

The first weeks after I had left the monastery to test my call to the solitary life had been ones of searing struggle rather than ecstatic experience. I soon learned (to my chagrin) that the difficulties I encountered in prayer could not be blamed on how others affected my life.

During those three months of my initial trial period, I lived in almost complete solitude, often having contact with other human beings only at Sunday liturgy. At this temporary abode, I had no car, no phone, not even a mailbox. A kindly neighbor would pick up my mail at the post office and leave it in the sacristy of the chapel near my hermitage. This was a cement-block structure with few windows, dark and cheerless. It was permeated with a dank odor from years without occupants. Since it had only minimal furnishings, and I had few resources, there seemed little I could do to brighten the place.

At the age of forty-seven, I was totally alone for the first time in my life. For many months I had struggled actively to get permission to live a hermit life, but when I finally achieved my goal, a frightening emptiness yawned before me.

One day I crouched before my makeshift altar, feeling vulnerable and lost. Nothing seemed either real or right. I took refuge in the concrete sensations of the moment. I felt my breath going in and out, my heart beating, my legs beginning to cramp. Shifting to a sitting position, I focused on a flickering candle.

I was awash with emotions of loss and grief, guilt and anxiety. I yearned to be comforted and assured that I had made the right decision. Instead, depression engulfed me. Some instinctive wisdom recognized that I should have expected this, that moving into solitude would be like embarking on a sea journey at night in a leaky rowboat without oars or tiller. I would be at the mercy of the wind, the waves, and the dark.

This imagery clarified the nebulous strangeness enveloping me. If I were on a foggy sea, it behooved me to at least plug the leaks in my frail craft. This meant recognizing my losses, accepting my grief, and praying out of my sadness.

74

The Psalms achieved new meaning as I recited them in my darkness and confusion:

Since you, O God, are my stronghold,
why have you rejected me?
Why do I go mourning
oppressed by the foe?

O send forth your light and your truth;
let these be my guide.
Let them bring me to your holy mountain,
to the place where you dwell. (Ps. 43, vv. 2-3)

Mountains, rocky and uninviting, literally encompassed me in this rugged section of Appalachia. Unwisely, I had chosen the dreariest months of the year for my first testing of solitary life — January through March. Grey skies, leafless trees, and barren ground surrounded the shanty where I lived. Barely five feet from the back steps of the hermitage, the land fell off into a rough ravine.

A scarcely discernible track zigzagged down from the edge. One day, desperate to escape the four walls, I risked the descent and stumbled upon a dirt road that paralleled a roaring, white-water stream called Mill Creek.

Exploring this tumultuous, ever-changing waterway became a part of my daily routine. As I followed its surging course around boulders and over steep falls, discovering strange and wonderful sights, I felt my aloneness even more keenly. There was no one with whom to share my thoughts and feelings.

I tasted the complete loneliness of solitude, reaching a zero point of personal desolation. I was totally alone but for an aloof Presence. With no one else available, my sheer need for relationship drove me to share my experiences, my discoveries, and my fears with this Strange One, so distant and yet closer than any other. Exploring the natural world around me, I simultaneously began to explore new possibilities of intimacy within myself.

There came a day when I noticed an old railroad trestle curving across the deep gorge carved by the rushing water, and I became obsessed with the idea of exploring the other, wilder side of Mill Creek. However, the bridge consisted of widely spaced ties, some of which were clearly rotting.

Frequently I would visit the bridge and stare along its curving length, only to turn back again to more familiar paths. Each time, I would notice something more . . . that it did seem to have solid foundations; that it did not shake despite the roaring waters at its base; and finally, that there were unmistakable signs that ATVs occasionally crossed it.

It was usable; it was there if I really wanted to cross it. Finally, on a mild day in early March, I set my booted foot on the first of the crumbling ties and set out. About midway across, I felt faint from the height; a dizzy sensation threatened to overwhelm me. I could turn back, but the return distance was roughly equal that to the other end of the trestle.

Trembling, I fixed my eyes on the far side, refusing to glance at the frothing water visible beneath my feet. Step by step, holding on to the thin air, I reached solid ground. Once my breathing returned to normal, I discovered a wilderness paradise. A deer track led me down a slope to a place where two waterfalls poured into a basin that shimmered, clear and cold, in the early spring sunlight.

I perched on a boulder, leaning my back against an overhanging hemlock. Wild rhododendron provided a natural enclosure. Directly across from me, a freshet stairstepped down the hillside. To my right, Mill Creek itself cascaded over a wide ledge of jutting rocks. A palpably Holy Presence pervaded this wilderness sanctuary.

Harmonies of rushing water filled the air. Birds twittered

76

and skimmed overhead. A sense of the Sacred invaded me, and I prayed with my eyes, my ears, my senses of touch and smell. For a long while, I merely absorbed the marvels of this mysterious abode of the Holy. Part of the delight that flooded me was a wonder that I, I had been led to this place by the God whom I was seeking . . . and who, I now realized, had also been seeking me!

When I finally retraced my steps across the trestle bridge, I felt both privileged and beloved. The Holy One who was calling me to risk all and follow new trails had shown His Face to me in that sacred glen.

After that, I returned often to my secret sanctuary, and each time the Mystery reached out to me anew. Then, just as spring was beginning to blossom, my three months' trial of hermit life came to an end, and I had to return to the monastery. I left enriched beyond my wildest imaginings, taking with me a conviction that if I persevered in solitude, the transparency to the Holy I yearned for would, some mysterious day, be given me.

My new dwelling place in Colt Run required a similar series of adjustments to solitude. Once I had unpacked my few household goods and established a rudimentary order around me, I could not escape the chaos within me. Without the established routines of the monastic day that had governed my life for over thirty years, I floundered, unable to distinguish my personal rhythms from the programmed ones.

It would take me years to discover the natural rhythms of my own body and spirit. At first, I defended myself against this too-much-freedom by following the daily schedule of prayer and work I had known in the monastery. Only slowly did I recognize and begin to react against this subtle tyranny. If solitude were to bear its promised fruit and make me as responsive to the Spirit of God as the grass waving in the field, I had to cease controlling my own life so rigidly.

My isolated situation included the deprivation of regular spiritual guidance, because experienced directors were hard to find in Appalachia. Whatever direction I required would have to be found within myself . . . or, more precisely, drawn from the Spirit dwelling in my deepest Center. Access to that core of my being was possible only through the most scrupulous honesty — a stark discipline.

As I struggled to find my way to the Kingdom within, I entered into a deepening communion with the world of nature surrounding my hermitage. Birds congregating at the feeder became vivid symbols of God's enduring care for all my needs. Groundhogs lumbering out of their burrows bespoke my bumbling efforts at contemplative prayer.

But it was the deer, fleeting gracefully along the rims of the ridges, that most clearly epitomized my yearnings for union with a God I occasionally glimpsed at the edges of my awareness. Despite their abundant numbers in the surrounding hills, I seldom saw deer near my house during the daylight hours. But I would hear them in the night and, come morning, would find hoofprints in my lawn.

Following deer trails through the woods, I would feel a secret communion with these shy, gentle creatures, so defenseless, so hunted. Yet one day I realized that I too was hunting them in my own way. I recognized that I wanted to exercise a subtle kind of dominion over the deer, that I desired to see them when and where and how I pleased. That is not the way with deer.

Deer appear or they don't. If you are in the right place at the right moment, you will see them, perhaps even very close at hand. But once you try to touch them, they flee. So, I discovered, it is with the comings and goings of the Spirit of God. If I wait, quietly going about the tasks of my day, I might glimpse a trace of His activity in my life, a subtle sign that He is just beyond the edge of my vision.

Occasionally, I might be led to a place where the veil will briefly lift, as on the day I crossed the trestle bridge. Although I can no longer return to that sacred glen, the experience of it prepared me to discover other natural places of wonder and worship.

One day, as I wandered a deer path through a springtime woods, I turned a corner and confronted a flame azalea in full bloom. It blazed in shimmering orange where sun rays touched its blossoms. Though no Voice thundered, I removed my shoes, for assuredly I was standing on Holy Ground. In the awesome silence, I could hear a rustling among the fallen leaves behind me, but I did not turn. I knew. I had found a place where even the deer knelt to pray.

XII

Beside Restful Waters

"BESIDE restful waters, O lead me!" I prayed with growing urgency. "Lead me to find your healing springs, O God, and deliver me from polluted wells."

In front of my cabin in Colt Run stood a picturesque stone well. A black pipe dropped over the edge to the water, scarcely six feet below ground level. Plastic hosing swung across space to a hole in the wall of my house. Even my inexperience had recognized that such a primitive arrangement boded trouble.

As the dry months of late summer wore on, the water level would drop alarmingly, and what water there was would turn murky. Heedless of neighbors' cautions, I continued to drink it, as well as wash with it. I deliberately ignored some vague physical distresses because I *wanted* this well to be, in fact, what I idealized it to be — the source of life-giving waters.

I was seized by the perennial fascination of water rising from the heart of the earth. Having a producing well was not only a physical necessity but also a spiritual one. Whenever I leaned over the rock rim and glimpsed the water shimmering in the dark below, I was mesmerized by visions of mysteries to be explored within my own soul.

My head and shoulders, haloed by the sun behind me, were mirrored in those still waters. A world beneath the surface

81

of daily concerns beckoned compellingly. Would I have the courage to drink from these frightening but inviting depths?

A Stranger from Galilee approached, dust-covered and thirsty, asking if I would let down my bucket. "If only you recognized God's gift, and who it is that is asking you for a drink," He said, "you would ask Him instead and He would give you living water so that you would never thirst again" (cf. John 4:10). I leaned against the cool stone, listening to the echoes as droplets plinked into the dark mirror below. Surely this well could not be anything but pure.

Early in my third summer, the kitchen faucet emitted a strange odor. When I lifted the flat rock from the rim of the well, gasoline fumes assailed me. How could this be? I knew that oil and natural gas had been pumped from these hills some years before, but by now, all operations in Colt Run had been shut down. Could one of the old pipelines crossing my backyard be leaking? Or the dump at the top of the ridge be leaching into the groundwater?

When I notified county and company authorities, they immediately took water samples. They confirmed the presence of gasoline but denied that it could come from the old oil installations. Then I picked up the nearby fuel can for my weed eater — almost all the gas was gone, apparently having leaked slowly through the rusted bottom and into the ground.

This answered one question but raised a host of others about the safety of the unsealed water supply I was using. If gasoline percolating into the ground yards away could leach into my well, what about contaminants from the small run only ten feet distant?

Further tests confirmed my worst fears. Bacterial matter in my well water exceeded the upper limits of safety, and it was declared unsafe for human consumption. Even boiling the water could not purify it sufficiently.

From then on, I fetched water via Radio Flyer wagon and

milk jugs from Jeanne and Jane's house, a quarter-mile down the road. I became intimately familiar with every rut and rock between their place and mine as, daily, I rattled and rolled along the road. After a while, their dog didn't even bother to bark at my deafening approach.

Sweating under the summer sun or slogging through mud puddles, I realized that I was doing what had been women's work from time immemorial. Even today, I reflected, nearly two-thirds of the world's population are dependent on water fetched by women, sometimes from incredible distances. In my mind, I pictured heavy jars, gracefully balanced on veiled heads, as well as scenes of dried-up riverbeds in drought-stricken areas.

I felt lucky. Safe water was freely available to me, but for many, water was a scarce and very precious commodity. I began to feel a kinship with my sisters who through patient and unremitting toil supplied their families with this most basic necessity. I felt part of an endless procession reaching back into the dim beginnings of human life on earth. With this new sense of connectedness, my impatience with my daily trek diminished.

Many people in these very hills surrounding me lacked a safe water supply. Most of the folk on the ridge depended on runoff from rain gathered into cisterns. Many, like me, had to get water from some more fortunate neighbor. This experience of poverty, this lack of conveniences I had once taken for granted, added a new dimension to my prayer life. I felt a deeper solidarity with all those who struggled for the bare necessities of life. Things I once considered indispensable became superficial.

An uncertain water supply had always ruled out such luxuries as an indoor toilet. Barely hidden among the trees stood my outhouse, doorless but not odorless. To avoid problems with a rather high water table in the holler, outhouses were built *up* the hillside. Mine was a good thirty feet above the house, accessible only by a steep path. How former tenants managed I could only guess. Maybe they were related to mountain goats?

At the steepest section, a few rocks formed some crude steps. This inspired me, and I launched a Major Improvement Project. Using broken cement blocks and flat stones that abounded in my "lawn," I started to construct a pathway of stepping stones which would enable me to travel dryshod to and from the outhouse.

This turned out to be more difficult than I had envisioned. Contrary to popular myth, rocks are very mobile objects. After each rain, they would be skewed about in the slippery mud. Those that remained had an unnerving tendency to rock in place, threatening my precarious balance. However, I was determined not to be a victim of vicious circumstances.

Lacking a shovel, I had to excavate the steps with a trowel. Soft, oozy mud turned hard as cement when dry, frustrating my efforts to scratch out places where I could snug in the rocks. At one spot, a stream flowed across the path for a day or so after every rain. Larger rocks had to be found to bridge this point. So I began to enlist my infrequent visitors in this project, promising, like St. Francis, a heavenly reward for each stone set in place.

Those who came found it to their personal advantage to contribute their time and energy! Company seldom stayed very long.

I had to find an alternative solution to the polluted well, but given my financial state, options were limited. There was a spring situated high on the ridge behind my house with no dwelling or pastureland above it. It had to be pure water, I assumed, so (foolishly) I did not have it tested before having it piped in. I employed a father-and-son team who used their backhoe to accomplish the feat of digging a ditch and laying pipe through rocky and mostly vertical terrain. They also built a holding tank at the spring site to capture its slow-rising waters.

I was pleased with this system. It required no electricity, because gravity alone provided ample pressure as the water descended from five hundred feet above the house. As long as the spring flowed strongly, the holding tank refilled continuously. This spring, however, depended more on rainfall for replenishment than I had realized.

Inevitably, a dry period caused the spring to diminish to a trickle. My prayer began to focus on the clouds — rain clouds! "Please send us drenching showers, Lord, to replenish this spring into which I have sunk almost all the money I have struggled to save for over two years."

My anxiety level increased even as the water table fell. In a moment of insight, I realized that I was more upset about the possibility that I had made an unwise decision than that I had no water. I had cherished a childish belief that my Good Father would always make things come out "right" even if I made foolish mistakes. My spring would be an unfailing source of pure water because I wanted it to be so. But it was not.

Within a few months, I was feeling poorly. Testing of the spring water confirmed my suspicions. Back to the red-wagon and milk-jug routine! Back, also, to the hard reality of admitting that I had make a costly mistake. It was a difficult moment for me, because Being Right was a supreme value, an important constituent of my self-esteem. However, facts implacably drove home the message that I, even I, could err in judgment, and that I would not be spared the price of my folly.

Accepting the formerly unacceptable proved a healing experience, and I moved closer to the restful waters of peace for which I yearned. I began to let go of my mindless compulsion to always be right. "To err was human," and was I not human? How relaxing to be just a human creature and not some infallible being beyond the mistakes of mere mortals! I smiled gently. This spring, which had made me sick with both anxiety and intestinal distress, had brought me face to face with my weaknesses, and, in accepting them, I discovered a new Strength.

The following year, I did what I should have done in the first place and applied for a permit to have a new well drilled. I had barely enough money to pay the drillers and figured I might have to install the new system piecemeal as I could afford it.

Once more I was being asked to step out onto thin air, trusting that I would be given whatever I needed when the moment came.

In early July, an impressive rig trundled into the field behind my house. The drilling site was limited to the one spot where the rig could be made operational. Volunteer "experts" had opined that water was likely to be found between sixty and eighty feet down. The cost would be ten dollars a foot for drilling, plus the expense for the pump, a new holding tank, and incidentals. I could just afford it.

As the drill spiraled downward, all signs were hopeful. Sand layers were met, blue shale shattered, caprock pierced. I left the drillers to go to town, assured that water would soon be gushing forth. I returned to an ominous silence and two dejected drillers slumped in the shade of the pine trees.

"We've gone down one hundred and forty feet, ma'am, and only found a trickle of water — less than a gallon an hour."

My heart plummeted lower than the drill bit as they further explained that the next depth at which water was likely to be found in this area was six hundred feet. The calculator in my head blinked red as it registered $6,000 — an amount far beyond my bank account.

It was agreed that they would stop drilling for the day while they gave me time to weigh the options: try another site (which meant $1,400 lost on this dry hole), drill deeper at the present site, or give it up altogether. There was the slight possibility that a vein of water had been temporarily sealed off by the rotary drill and *might* break through during the next twenty-four hours. They told me that, for an additional charge of only a hundred dollars, they could try a procedure called "fracking" the next morning. But they could guarantee nothing.

As the men drove off, I went out to where the rig towered

over the dry hole. With my ear against the piping, I could detect the faint tinkle of water far down the shaft. Much too slow to be of any use, I knew. I laid my hands on the pipe and prayed to the God of springs and fountains to send water into this empty well. My recent experiences with water did little to reinforce my faith.

I scratched a cross on the drill shaft and retired for the night. Early the next morning, I scurried out to the rig and listened hopefully. Only a slow dripping echoed up the shaft.

I called a friend who lived on the ridge. She had a remarkable gift for detecting underground water, so I asked her to come down and give me an "assessment." She walked slowly over the entire property, trying to sense where a vein of water might be located. All the likely spots registered negative. The only place she detected water was where the rig stood.

She and her family were still with me when the drilling team returned. Next my pastor arrived. Our prayers were drowned out by a high-pitched whine as the "fracking" process began. The men started to force air down the shaft. The theory was that if a vein of water were nearby, the pressure might crack the rock, causing the water to flow into the well hole. I caught my breath when the machine was suddenly silenced.

Cautiously the men began releasing the trapped air. At first all I heard was the whistle of escaping gases. Then I began to detect something else. Was it merely the rattling of the drill bit, or was it — could it be — gurgling water? Anxiously I watched the men on the rig. A slight relaxation of tension, then tentative smiles, and finally arms upraised in triumph as a rushing, bubbling music emerged from the well hole. We had found water!

The vein proved to be strong, providing pure, soft water in exuberant abundance. As one of the drillers said, I not only had a good well, I had a *great* well! Testing proved that the water was of excellent quality. I still breathe a prayer of humble gratitude whenever I turn on a spigot in the house and clean water spurts forth. A risk, however reluctantly I had embraced it, had resulted in healing waters flowing not only into my house but also into my spirit.

Then I learned that the new environmental code required that a septic system be installed — another costly venture. I studied my savings account. The tiny amount reminded me of the oil the widow of Sidon had in the bottom of her jug. Yet, somehow, it had stretched to meet the expenses of the well, thanks to an anonymous benefactor whose gift had arrived along with the bills.

Perhaps my "jug" would not go empty so long as I was willing to risk pouring out its contents? The only suitable site for the leach bed that aerated the outflow from the septic tank was (naturally!) the field that served as my front yard. So, a few months after my well became operational, a bulldozer was again at work digging and scraping. By the time my third winter in the holler began, I no longer needed to make the trek to the outhouse, and the path I had constructed with so much toil fell into disuse — a labor gladly lost!

It was too late in the year to sow new grass, so I went through another season of Major Mud. Yard, field, and drive lay raw and brown throughout the winter months. But the dreary sight attested that my prayers had been answered.

One day, shortly before Holy Week, something in the tumbled ground of the leach bed caught my eye. Donning my boots, I picked my way through stones and mud to the place where blades of green were thrusting toward the blue sky. They had a yellowish tinge, as if they had had to struggle through several feet of earth. There, not far from the gurgling run, daffodils were forming buds. Uprooted, buried, scattered, these hardy survivors prophesied green pastures and restful waters.

XIII

Halving the Last Loaf

HUMMING softly to myself, I moved about the kitchen, assembling ingredients for honey-wheat bread. I loved the process of baking my own bread — kneading the sticky mass into a smooth dough, feeling the living yeast beginning to respond under my hands, observing the miracle as the small lump expanded, and above all, smelling the ineffable fragrance of baking bread as my loaves browned in the oven.

A fresh breeze wafted through the open window, mellow with the warmth of spring. Hummingbirds fluttered around the feeder hung outside the window above the sink. I noted that my supply of whole wheat flour was nearly depleted and added it to my grocery list.

I was rhythmically kneading the dough when my phone rang. What now? I threw a towel over the sticky mess on the table and attempted to rub off the bits of dough clinging to my fingers. Sighing at this intrusion into my peaceful morning, I crossed the room to the phone.

The caller was someone I had not heard from since I first moved into my hermitage a couple of years before. Instinctively, I sensed this was no casual call. I listened to a rapid-fire description of multiple mishaps: slow recovery from major heart surgery, loss of a job, threatened eviction, missed car payments

. . . and now, a lawsuit. Jeb needed money for a lawyer because he risked unfair conviction in small claims court.

Graphically he described the humiliation of being finger-printed, getting a mug shot, and standing with other suspected criminals in the alien atmosphere of a police station.

Cautiously I asked how much he needed. The lawyer required a hundred dollars up front before he would accept the case. Jeb was innocent; he had proof that he had paid for the item he was accused of stealing. But he needed a person with knowledge of court procedures to successfully present his case.

"Isn't there some provision for indigent defendants?" I inquired. No, this lawyer — the good one he needed — didn't take such cases. I frowned as I listened to the anxious voice on the phone. I knew Jeb and trusted his story. But one hundred dollars? That was exactly half the amount in my checking account.

How soon did he need the money? It had to be in the lawyer's hands within three days. Then I heard another Voice, quiet but imperative: "Give it to him." I recognized that more than a loan of a hundred dollars was at stake. My future was in jeopardy.

I could refuse this request in the name of prudence and good sense. Most people would advise me that Jeb's problems were not my responsibility. But the Lord was telling me other-wise. At this moment, Jeb was my "bundle," an old Quaker term for a concern specifically destined for you. To refuse. . . .

I heard myself promising to put a check in the mail that day. Jeb's fervent gratitude and his pledge to repay me within six months echoed in my ear as I replaced the receiver. The gratitude I believed; the pledge I doubted.

When I resumed my interrupted kneading, a story from the life of St. Clare jogged my memory. One day there was only one loaf of bread left in her monastery to feed the fifty sisters soon to gather for their noon meal. Furthermore, the portress had just informed her that some brothers were at the front door, asking for food. What to do?

Clare directed the portress to divide their one loaf and give half to the brothers. The rest she was to portion out among the waiting sisters. Mumbling to herself that expecting another miracle of the loaves and fishes was outrageous, the sister did as she was told. History records that that half-loaf provided generous servings for every single nun.

The lesson was clear to me. I could not deny my brother. Nor would I ever lack what I truly required. When I needed it, the bread I was now about to cast upon the waters would come back to me. I wrote out the check for Jeb, wincing as I noted that this left exactly $99.46 in my account.

Because I needed to get the check in the mail as soon as possible, I trekked up the hill to my mailbox on the ridge, enjoying the twenty-minute climb in the fresh spring air. Yesterday's mail was still in my box, and I glanced casually through the few letters. Nothing particularly exciting, I thought.

When I got back to the house, I settled down on the sunny porch to open my mail. A check fell out of one of the envelopes, a check for one hundred dollars! I stared at it in amazement. "Your timing, Lord, is utterly fantastic," I murmured. Just then the aroma of baking bread wafted through the door. I jumped up to rescue the golden loaves from the oven and wondered with whom I would be asked to share them.

Once again I had experienced how my Faithful God provided for my every need, even forestalling a single day of worry. "Enough, then, of worrying about tomorrow. Let tomorrow take care of itself. Seek first his kingship over you, his way of holiness, and all these things will be given you besides" (Matt. 6:34,33).

"Seek first his kingship. . . ." This had been the "word" I had received during a discernment retreat I had made shortly after moving to my hermitage in Colt Run. Only a few months in "the world" had made me aware of how unrealistic was my plan to live a contemplative lifestyle with no source of steady income. My small nest egg was melting away with frightening rapidity.

Perhaps I should find a job? Yet I had not left the monastery to enter the marketplace. I was seeking solitude so that I would have even more time to devote to prayer and contemplative listening. During this retreat, my director gave me a koan, a paradoxical statement, to consider: "Solitude is togetherness." It seemed to have no direct relevance to the question I was pondering, but I obediently "sat" with it.

In the stillness, I recognized that if my life in Colt Run was not to become a lie and an escape, I had to develop a welcoming heart toward all; I had to learn to stand with open — perhaps empty — hands before whomever life would put in my path. Thomas Merton had noted that the traditional virtues of hermit life are, almost paradoxically, compassion and hospitality.

I felt challenged to an openness of heart and house far beyond my capacities or even desires. Poverty of place and circumstance, I realized, were to recreate me so I could discover a tremendous inner freedom. I would experience this liberty only when — and if — I was willing to let go of all the normal securities of life, "necessities" such as a steady income, insurance, and retirement benefits.

The demand was that I embrace a totally crazy, utterly foolhardy dependence on God alone. I was to live only for the day and to trust that bread for the next meal would arrive when the next meal did. And if it didn't? Well, then, I would be given strength to deal with that, too.

When I had moved into the empty house in Colt Run, I had felt a kinship with Clare of Assisi. I felt that I was reliving in my time and place the experience she and her sister, Agnes, had known when they had walked into the bare stone building at San Damiano with nothing but their trust in God for food and raiment.

In my personal call to be a Clare, I perceived a continuity with the Franciscan experience through the centuries — the same charism, the same radical poverty. The answer to the question of my retreat welled up spontaneously. I heard Clare say to me in 1989 what she had written to Agnes of Prague in 1234: "You've chosen to walk the path which Jesus walked for you. So live by your trust in Him and know that His way is true."

Trust! This was what God required of me. "There where clinging to things ends, there God begins to be," Meister Eckhart had said succinctly. If I truly wished to encounter the Living God, I had to put myself totally in His hands with no material concerns to weigh me down. I gave up the struggle with common sense and chose, as many had before me, the challenge to live literally the injunction of the Sermon on the Mount: "You cannot give yourself to God and money" (Matt. 6:24).

Visions of the lilies of the field and the birds of the air danced in my head. "If God can clothe in such splendor the grass of the field, which blooms today and is thrown on the fire tomorrow, will he not provide much more for you, O weak in faith! Stop worrying, then, over such questions like, 'What are we to eat, or what are we to drink, or what are we to wear?' . . . Your heavenly Father knows all that you need. Seek first his kingship over you, his way of holiness, and all these things will be given you besides" (Matt. 6:30-33).

I returned to Colt Run with no guarantee for my future except this: if the Lord was calling me to live a contemplative life in solitude, all I needed would be provided. Why then was I surprised to find that a load of firewood had been dumped, gratis, in my front yard during my absence? Or astonished when a box of used winter clothing was delivered to my door?

A week later an envelope with no return address arrived,

and when I opened it, a cashier's check for two hundred dollars fluttered onto my lap. I was overwhelmed. And my wonder grew as, month after month, a two-hundred-dollar check faithfully turned up in my mailbox. I have never learned who my mysterious benefactor is. The check comes from a city where I have no relatives or close acquaintances. Sometimes the blank for the remitter's name is filled in "St. Francis"!

Four years later, this Anonymous Donor is still surprising me. Since I don't know who to thank, or whether to expect another such check, each new donation is like a message from God Himself, assuring me that He *will* provide all that I need and more. Someone is sharing their bread with me. My challenge is to share mine with others.

XIV

Weathering the Weather

GENTLE April breezes stirred young leaves as the sun sank behind the western ridge of the holler. I glanced from my window to see my neighbors, Jeanne and Jane, accompanied by their dog, Mateo, strolling up my drive. It was my turn to host our weekly sharing and supper together. After a last check on the oven, I joined them for our prayer service.

I had planned a celebration of spring, my third in the holler. We offered our final prayers on the hillside as we knelt around a symbol of spring especially dear to me, a clump of blooming trillium. The lily-white blossoms had opened only that day. Rather than pick them for my altar, I preferred to honor them (and their Creator) in the beauty of their woodsy habitat.

Our prayer ended, we lingered in the warm evening air, admiring the various signs of advancing spring. I was just showing off some new bulbs that were sprouting when a gust of cold wind surprised us. I looked up to see greenish clouds boiling over the ridge across the valley.

"That looks like a tornado!" Jane shouted.

"That color means hail!" shrieked Jeanne.

With the wind rising to a howl behind us, we dashed for the house. Once inside, Jane yelled frantically, "Where's the safest place?"

"Under the steps, I guess," I shouted, as I struggled to close and bolt the heavy door. A blinding torrent of hail roared up the holler, and I ran to close windows. The storm struck so forcefully that I feared the glass would break. There was a sharp snapping, and the house shook. Then the lights went out.

In the sudden dark, I could hear the furious wind whipping rain through cracks in the roof and walls. I grabbed a handy flashlight and looked about. A glistening cascade of water was dancing on the altar. Even as I fumbled for some buckets, I heard the raging of the wind diminish, leaving only the drumming of a steady downpour.

In the relative quiet, a voice quavered, "Is it safe?" Turning, I beheld one friend crawling out of the bathtub, clutching the dog, and the other trying to disentangle herself from the jumble of boots and rugs beneath the steps. I was shaken by a mix of reactions — laughter, anger that my friends had left me to cope alone, and shock that, in my witless concern to close windows, I might have been killed.

The worst of the storm was clearly past, and we tried to determine the damage. Through the pouring rain, I could see that a huge pine had been snapped on the hillside near the house, tearing down phone and power lines as it fell. Suddenly I realized that my cat, Merton, was out there somewhere.

My friends deterred me from dashing out into the deluge, assuring me that Merton had undoubtedly found a safe place. I wondered if there was any such thing during a storm so furious, but heeded their advice to wait. My friends were right: soon a very wet, very indignant white cat mewed at the door and stalked in without a glance for me when I rushed to open it.

As soon as the rain let up a little, Jeanne and Jane left to assess the damage to the buildings on their property. I donned my raincoat to survey the situation on my premises. Hail the size of golf balls was heaped about. On the hillside, the trillium lay slivered, blossoms limp as used tissue.

96

My investigation proved that the brunt of the storm had passed above my house but that homes on the top of the ridge had taken a severe beating. Through the twilight, I could hear the whine of chain saws as homeowners and work crews began to clear roads and remove fallen trees from downed power lines.

The demise of my trillium was certainly a minor disaster amid the major damage caused by this storm, and no pictures of them appeared among the dramatic photos splashed across our weekly paper. But I grieved for them as for personal friends whose beauty I would miss the rest of that spring.

Living in close proximity to nature, vulnerable to all the vicissitudes of the weather, I was developing an affinity with every nuance of the changing seasons. Each month had its special flavor, its own color, fragrance, and emotion.

February was brown and smelled of decay; April, fresh with new green; June, lush and sweetly perfumed. I observed the seasonal advances, one day at a time, through the windows of my prayer alcove. Early in March, I began to scan the ridges for that subtle shift when brown sheathes fell from overwintering buds and a blush of deep red suffused the hillsides.

Slowly a mist of greenery gathered about the feet of the tall trees as briars began to leaf out. Soon the vibrant redbuds lighted the hills, followed not long after by the bride of spring, the flowering dogwood. I delighted to see the sunny daffodils reappear and began to assess the quality of the year's berry crop by the flowering brambles along the roadside.

Although the spring was a constant revelation, it did not take me by surprise. I had observed its arrival, stage by stage, and had been changed even more than the land by the process. I had seen the crocuses in the ell of my house poise on the verge of blooming through long days of freezing rain until one fine day, touched by the sun, the petals unfurled.

From them I learned something about awaiting the right moment, about enduring patiently the vicissitudes of prayer, the ebb and flow of energy, and long periods of doubt. I came to recognize a rhythmic pulse of the Spirit that led me, through the depression and loneliness that frequently chilled my solitude, into a new warmth of companionship and contentment.

Instead of lamenting these alternating states, I began to look upon them as indicators of change, of progress. Transformation was not a comfortable process, and I tended to resist it. I frequently felt trapped in my hermitage by mud and dripping clouds until I chose to explore the areas within myself that loneliness uncovered. There I discovered some spring bulbs, little sprouts of courage and joy, pushing aside the tangled weeds of my inner landscape, and I learned how to clear the ground for their blossoming.

My first spring had found me emerging like a groundhog from a burrow where I felt my deepest self had been hibernating for years uncounted. The sunlight dazed me, this revealing light that enabled me to see myself as if for the first time.

I was no longer among a crowd that obscured my personal shape but very alone with grasses not yet green. I had survived winter in a hermitage despite dire predictions from friends and relatives. And now I was standing on the verge of a new freedom as chains of fear and inexperience fell from me.

Who, I wondered, could comprehend the countless victories won? The numberless small triumphs that consisted of nothing more than things like learning to shop after thirty years, during which time I never saw the inside of a supermarket? Would anyone understand what it meant to learn to do such ordinary things as go to a laundromat, buy some stamps, open a checking account?

I still had to suppress small terrors each time I got behind the wheel of a car. But the point was, I *did* drive — not only along the rugged back roads but also on highways and through whooshing city traffic whenever necessary. The time I had found myself stranded on the interstate had not proven so traumatic after all. A providential angel had come along, and a lost muffler was not the total disaster it had seemed.

Little by little, like spring in its surging, I felt myself growing into a new sense of competency, a "can-do" attitude that enabled me to tackle all the problems which weather and circumstances threw my way. Not always with immediate success, however.

As summer heat took over and I was compelled to leave my front door open for ventilation, the lack of a screen door allowed more than my cat to go freely in and out of my hermitage. An occasional butterfly I did not mind, but the wasps and flies were definitely a nuisance.

My doorway, broad and low, had unusual dimensions, so no inexpensive, readymade door would solve the problem. My first solution was a homemade screen door that I had to lift in and out of place because there was no room for it to swing on hinges. Unfortunately, it was so heavy that I strained my back trying to move it.

When a friend was knocked clear off the steps and nearly brained by the tumbling door, I knew it was not the ideal solution to my problem. Some brilliant individual suggested that I hang nylon screening across the doorway with Velcro. Voila! Merton quickly learned to pull aside a corner to let himself in and out, but flying creatures were effectively thwarted.

Advancing summer brought its particular joys and challenges. Thick foliage screened my little house from the road so effectively that some prospective visitors missed my place entirely. I enjoyed the privacy the thick growth afforded, as well as the shade that kept me relatively cool while others sweltered.

Summer also gave me a chance to explore the holler. One day I followed a cow path through rising pastureland, emerging at last on a barren height with a panorama of wooded ridges in all directions. I surveyed hills unfolding toward the horizon with no sign of human habitation except a blinking tower on a distant peak.

With such vistas unrolling in beauty, how could one be poor? A breeze swept through my hair as I sat enthralled, hawks dipping and swooping in the sky above me. A deer emerged briefly from the edge of the woods below and then melted into the shadows again. The silence was alive with the humming of insects, piercing birdcalls, and the vast breathing of the wind.

I felt a communion with the Holy that compassed and calmed me. All my struggles were worthwhile when seen from the vantage of this High Place. I was filled with exhilaration, a feeling of having met and conquered numberless foes, a certainty that I would overcome in my quest for the God who dwelt in these hills.

My confidence was soon challenged when a dark cloud passed across the sun. A thunderstorm was brewing, and the highest hill in the area was not the best place to be. As large drops began to fall, I scooted and slid down the rough track.

It was raining heavily by the time I reached flat ground. Braving the cows that were grazing in my path, I took refuge in a collapsing corncrib, finding one corner where the roof still covered the rafters.

A bolt of lightning struck so close that the wind of it literally blew the hat from my head. "Lord," I gasped through chattering teeth, "did You have to give me such a dramatic sign of Your Power and Presence?"

Late summer — nights brilliant with stars overhead, and myriads of fireflies flickering soundlessly in the fields. Sitting on my porch as dusk deepened, I listened as the busy sounds of day died away and a tranquil chorus of cicadas and crickets struck up. Only rarely now did I catch the insistent whistle of the whippoorwill that had heralded spring.

The sweet fragrance of mown fields drifted on the air, reminding me that harvest was at hand. I had so much for which to be grateful: another year in solitude drawing toward the vibrancy of autumn; a summer of storms survived; the prospect of a life rich beyond anything I deserved spreading before me.

Into my contented musings slipped concerns about gathering the winter wood supply. The open cellar area beside the house had been roofed over, and now I could enjoy the ultimate luxury of bringing in my firewood without even stepping outdoors. It was a large, dry place — but alas, largely empty.

Once again my vulnerability and weakness bore down on me. I did not own — and was terrified to use — a chain saw. I was hopelessly inept and definitely dangerous with an axe in my hands. How would I fill that cellar? Just as I was gearing up for a grand bout of anxiety, a soft whoo-whoo in the pine by the porch startled me.

Peering into the shadows, I discerned the distinctive shape of a downy owl. It glided closer on silent wings. Landing, it gravely regarded me with wise golden eyes. I felt singularly "beheld" and ever so gently chided for my lack of faith. Perhaps owls as well as doves can be messengers of the Spirit?

My new woodshed did fill up with kindling and split logs, some donated, some laboriously cut and gathered from the ridge in company with Jane and Jeanne. By the time freezing temperatures again visited the holler, I and my house were well prepared for stormy blasts and bleak days.

The glorious gala of autumn, for which all the trees had dressed in crimson and gold for their final fling, had played across the ridges ringing my hermitage. The poignancy of the season pierced me — the stark necessity of letting go one more time and surrendering all that had "clothed" me during months of sunshine had to be accepted all over again.

The signature of God, written in the dark limbs of stripped trees, spread boldly across the hills. For everything and everyone there is a season: a time to receive, and a time to give; a time to do, and a time to wait; a time for grief, and a time for glory.

XV

Quilt Frames and Computers

AS I manuevered the long cartons up the twisting stairway to my loft bed- and work-room — still a tricky ascent after three years — a cherished but almost forgotten memory came surging back to me. In my mind's eye, I could see my grandmother smiling gently as she bent over her quilt frame, set up near a bay window filled with African violets.

One day, just before I left home to enter a monastery, she asked me to help her work on the quilt currently stretched on her frames. It had a white top covered with cross-stitch designs in moss green. I put in a few awkward stitches, managing to prick my finger and leave an indelible mark on the quilt.

Perhaps that memory underlay my determination to learn quilting when I moved into solitary life. My first paid sewing job was, amazingly, making an appliquéd quilt top for an elderly quilter whose rheumatic hands no longer could ply a needle.

Later, I bought some books and began to learn the techniques of machine piecing. It was fascinating to see a design emerge from squares and strips and triangles of cloth. A friend invited me to attend a quilt workshop at a nearby craft center. This experience deepened my determination to become a quilter.

Now I was about to assemble a quilting frame on which I

103

could stretch the first full-sized top I had ever pieced. Undaunted by the fact that I didn't know a bolt from a wing nut, I laid out the variety of screws, brackets, and wood strips that had tumbled from the cartons onto the bedroom floor.

I implemented the step-by-step instructions, carefully matching names to kit pieces and following the drawings, until, finally, my frame sat up on its wobbly legs. A profound sense of satisfaction filled me, not just because I had assembled the quilt frame, but because I now had one of my own. Something had come full circle.

My plans for using my quilting skills to help support myself were considered unrealistic by my many unsolicited advisors. Better I stay with the part-time job as parish secretary that I had held for a couple of years, they said. But I had become less and less comfortable with working away from the hermitage, even one day a week.

Contemplative prayer, as I experienced it, flowed best when I could maintain a daily rhythm of silence and solitude. Trusting blindly that the Lord would provide if I but sought Him sincerely, I announced my intention to resign even this meager bit of steady income.

That very week a quilting cooperative opened a training center in town and started seeking recruits. My application for membership was quickly accepted, and I began classes. And with them, a new stage in the school of grace.

Patience had never been my strong suit, nor was I a perfectionist. Now I learned that one sixteenth-inch stitch could make or mar the quality of a finished piece. I ripped more than I stitched, muttering through clenched teeth, "As ye sew, so shall ye rip." Frequently I despaired of ever producing a piece of work acceptable for sale in a co-op that had the highest reputation.

When the fourth star I pieced, with infinite care for precise matching, turned out to measure less than the requisite eighteen inches from point to point, my cup of frustration over-flowed. Throwing the useless piece, on which I had lavished eight hours of intense work, into the cupboard, I began a frenzy of housework. I stumped about, dumping the ashes from the wood stove, refilling the woodbox, wrestling with my disappointment over my ineptitude at a craft I had thought I loved.

Finally I returned to my sewing table. Something deep within me rebelled at trying the project once again. I was only wasting my time. But almost automatically my hand reached out for my rotary cutter, and I carefully aligned my ruler on the material spread across the cutting board. Squinting to read the seven-eighths-inch markings, I painstakingly sliced another strip of cotton to begin yet one more star.

This time, although I had to rip out stitches repeatedly, I sewed with a strange sense of peace. My anger had evaporated, leaving me with a peaceful sense that a finished — or even perfect — product was not my goal; submitting to the discipline of my craft was the real reason why I was sewing.

I had begun quilting classes planning to generate income. Now I realized that what were to be honed were not my sewing skills but rather the rough spots in my character.

Could I learn to undo, rip, and revamp a quilt piece until I could take total pride in the work of my hands? Could I respect the slow, arduous process of developing new skills and let go of my compulsion to bring a thing to completion as quickly as possible? Was there something more to this process than just finishing a piece of work and getting paid for it? Was there, perhaps, something intrinsically holy about putting my whole self into producing something beautiful, a quality piece of work, perfect for its own sake?

The frustrating discipline of ripping and resewing, of striving for a seemingly unattainable perfection, was beginning to change me. It began to affect every aspect of my life, even my prayer. In essence, I was becoming a bit more humble. I no longer assumed that whatever I did would be acceptable just because I produced it. There were standards beyond the ones I had previously set for myself.

I was being challenged to develop a new level of skill, and the only way to do so was by failing and learning from that failure, over and over. A profound shift began within me. I became gentler, more tolerant of failure in myself and others. I also learned that no mistake is totally irredeemable. With a little patience and ingenuity, with a willingness to "rip" and start over, almost any error could be either remedied or grown through. Failing was a necessary part of the process of life. This realization lifted a burden from me — that of always having to do everything right.

I didn't even have to be right before God. When my "seams" didn't match and my life was not fitting together, I could take it to Him and learn what needed to be remedied. I didn't have to be totally finished before I came to prayer — prayer was the time when my frazzled edges could be smoothed and the seemingly haphazard pattern of my day could be put into perspective.

I gained something else as well — a growing respect for all the tasks of my daily life. Perhaps washing dishes was not, strictly speaking, a craft, but that chore could be done beautifully and for its own sake. I learned to wash the plates and glasses caringly, not just to get them clean, but to enjoy the sparkle of sunlight on clear glass and savor the sheen of polished silver.

My quilting skills eventually developed (along with my patience and humility!) so that I became a contributing member of the local quilt cooperative. I enjoyed my weekly contact with the feisty, industrious Appalachian women who were the moving spirit of this venture. And I was proud to help weave a craft from these mountains into the rich tapestry of American life.

Becoming a craftsperson was a way of life. So was being a writer. When I first moved into solitude, creative writing had proven impossible for me. All my energies had been absorbed by adjustment and change. The only writing I did was in my daily journal, sorting out and seeking to understand the events of each day.

The need to write hounded me, but when I tried to do it, I found my thoughts flitting in fifty odd directions, and whatever I produced was scattered and shallow. This profoundly disappointed and disturbed me. For one of the underlying reasons I had moved into solitude was so that I might have more time and inner space for writing.

During my years in the monastery, I had written and published over one hundred articles and poems, mostly on religious subjects or my love of nature. I regarded myself as a poet — untrained, perhaps, but gifted enough to occasionally break into print.

Now I found my days crowded with the tasks of daily living, chores that had once been shared with others. But alone, there was only me to wash and clean and cook and fill the woodbox and write letters and do the shopping. . . . A moment of truth dawned during a retreat I made about three years after I moved to Colt Run. It wasn't the housework that kept me from writing; it was the sheer honesty demanded by the craft that deterred me.

I admitted to myself that I always found time for whatever I really wanted to do. There was, in truth, plenty of time for writing — what I lacked was courage. I shrank from writing because I did not want to give myself away. A lifelong habit of concealing my feelings, my fears, and my weaknesses kept me spinning my wheels whenever I considered writing the one thing I knew I had to write: the story of what God was doing in my life.

Encouragement from others only deepened my sense of

guilt. Like Jonah, my favorite non-prophet, I wanted to run from the Voice of God sending me to proclaim His message of providential love and mercy. But finally, like Jonah, I found myself in the belly of a whale, a life-process that was swallowing me whole. I was being overwhelmed by too many unexplored feelings, too much unexpressed experience.

Like a woman nearing the term of her pregnancy, I was heavy with unspoken words, thoughts, emotions. I could feel the movement and life of the child within — it was time to begin the birthing. I made a resolution that my Lenten penance that year would be to write poetry every day. Not a day was to go by that I would not sit, for at least half an hour, with my notebook on my knee and wrestle with putting some glimmer of truth into words.

I kept my resolution. It was a small but graced return to the struggle that the craft of writing demanded of me. It was a tiny, tentative step toward speaking my truth. The poems I wrote during that period were mostly nature pieces, descriptions of the slow birthing of spring; of sunny warmth overcoming the chill death of winter. I seldom wrote directly of myself or my feelings. I couldn't. A lifetime of concealment imprisoned me.

But slowly, brick by brick, I began to dismantle the walls I had erected. The poems gradually filled my notebook, and shyly I dared to share one or another with trusted friends. Finally, I risked typing them out, polishing them up for possible presentation to a wider audience that I assumed would be critical, perhaps even hostile.

I was fortunate to meet someone who was qualified to critique the work I was doing, and I submitted my poetry for her judgment. Much to my surprise, her response was generous, enthusiastic, and insightful. I walked two feet above the ground for weeks afterward.

A year after I returned to writing poetry, I imposed a harder discipline on myself. For the first hour after prayer each day, I would sit at my typewriter and tap the keys. That hour would be devoted to writing about my experience of moving into hermit life. For the first few weeks, I seldom wrote more than a paragraph a day; occasionally I might peck out a page.

Much of the time I spent staring into space, paralyzed by a subconscious conflict between my need to tell the story and my horror of self-revelation. I managed to break the impasse by adopting an objective stance, a journalist's reporting style, recounting the facts as if they had happened to someone else.

The result was stilted, dull, uninspired. I knew I was capable of better than this. But maybe it would do; perhaps the facts were enough. A good friend patiently plowed through the hundred pages I had written with such labor and told me flat out, "No one will ever want to read this. You can never get this published."

I felt extremely angry. Didn't he appreciate what I was trying to do? Why was he judging my work according to what he thought it should be? I retrieved my precious manuscript in a defensive huff, not very successfully hiding my hurt and disappointment. Only weeks later could I admit what I had known all along — that he was right *and* that I owed him a debt of gratitude for his willingness to tell me the truth.

The jumbled, run-on narrative, without drama or affect, was not going to interest anyone or, more importantly at this stage, excite a publisher. Discouraged, I set it aside and occupied myself in writing up talks on St. Clare to give in the occasional workshops I presented, and in pursuing my research (via survey letters) on hermit life. But a gnawing unease kept me restlessly returning to the discarded manuscript.

Finally I hit upon the plan of writing short vignettes, brief stories of some of the more dramatic incidents I had experienced since moving to Colt Run. I poured my story-telling skills into the effort and had soon assembled a group of five vivid incidents as a core for my proposed book. Once again I offered them to my friend to critique, and once again he challenged me to write not just what had happened but how it had affected and changed me.

What! Make a general confession on paper? Give away my deepest feelings, many of which, I had to admit, I didn't really know myself? A critique from a publisher to whom I had submitted the sample chapters confirmed my friend's suggestion. Where were the fresh insights? The new visions that one looked for from someone who had chosen the alternative lifestyle of a hermit?

"They are there," I fumed. "Can't my readers see them?" Apparently not. I was faced with another major revision, and I might have shirked the task had not a computer fallen into my life at this critical juncture. Thanks to the marvelous generosity of the Franciscan friars, a computer they were replacing was earmarked for a hermitage in West Virginia. It arrived complete with printer, programs, and paper.

After an initial period of intimidation, I began to experiment with the word-processing capabilities of the amber screen in front of me. I typed in one of my stories. Reviewing the text slowly and thoughtfully, I recognized places where moments of insight or emotion could be woven into the story. I was gripped by an excitement that helped me overcome my inbuilt reluctance about self-revelation. As I worked, I realized that I was finally finding my own "voice" in this uncomfortable genre. But that did not mean that I now wrote without struggle.

Often I would come to a sticking point, and rather than write what I really felt, I would veer off into another bit of description. When I would reread my work the next day, I would start to recognize those places. The computer screen made it easier to revise, to rework a sentence repeatedly as I groped toward clarifying my own understanding and then for the words to express it truthfully.

This discipline, which other writers have likened to a general confession, scoured my soul. With cruel clarity, I saw my escapes into diffuse language, vague generalities, even lively imagery that disguised rather than revealed. The struggle for straightforward expression became a major conversion experience. I had to acknowledge that I did not know myself or what moved me mainly because I did not *want* to. I much preferred the world of fuzzy feelings, experienced but unexpressed and, therefore, unexamined.

My hours before the computer became a dialogue, a challenge, a confrontation. Would I dare to tell my truth? More crucially, would I dare to *know* my truth? At times, it was a sweaty struggle to pull up one more self-revealing word from my inner darkness and display it on the glowing screen. But each time I did so, I found release and new freedom.

Some of my articles on St. Clare were published by religious periodicals, and a few poems were accepted as well. The encouragement engendered was like an updraft under my fledgling wings, and I turned to my computer with renewed energy. I gained enough courage to query half-a-dozen publishers about my proposed book of vignettes on my hermit life.

The May day I received a call from a publisher willing to give me a contract was glorious beyond belief. Dazedly I wandered from the phone to my worship space and sank back on my heels. "Lord," I whispered, "did You hear?" A great, warm smile enveloped me.

Writing and quilting together generate about one-fourth of my annual income, although they consume three-fourths of my time. Clearly the major gain from these crafts is not monetary. If quilting demands humility, the craft of writing imposes integrity. And both bestow the gift of liberty, one of the major graces of hermit life.

XVI

A Garden Place Grows Slowly

DOMINATING the view from my back window is a weathered construction of rotting boards and rusted tin. Whatever its original purpose in the dim past, this shed has become the repository of junk from numerous tenants preceding my arrival in Colt Run. Its collapse appears imminent, but somehow it remains upright, listing toward the north a bit more each year.

I labeled it the Magic Shed, not the least of its marvels being the fact that it continues to stand. Somehow, the four tree trunks that form its corners stubbornly refuse to surrender, although the rafters are disintegrating, and rivers of runoff scour their foundations.

The Magic Shed harbored an amazing collection of discards, ranging from bags of nails and cement (now rock hard) to a copper-bottom frying pan and a glass candleholder, still unchipped. My forays under its rusting roof were always brief, for I feared — with good reason — that it could collapse on my head, or that a snake might slither out from under a pile of debris.

Shortly after I moved to Colt Run, I determined that one of my first beautification projects would be the removal of this unsightly structure. But I continually put off my plan because

I had to tend to repairs or improvements of more immediate concern — such as rebuilding the chimney of the house, jacking up floorboards when a joist broke, and replacing broken pipes.

Four years have passed, and the Magic Shed still stands, uglier and more decrepit than ever. I look at it with a mixture of antipathy and affection. I can't help but admire such stubborn determination to hold together despite the ravages of time and weather. There is something to be said for a fixed foundation, for digging in for the long haul.

When I first came to Colt Run, my situation looked very unstable: I had an untested ability to live long-term in solitude, no steady income, no assurance that I could continue living here rent-free. Four years later, not much has changed.

My condition is just as insecure. I have no guarantees regarding my tenancy beyond verbal agreements; my income is unpredictable; my commitment to solitude is lived one day at a time. What did change was how I felt about insecurity and a precarious future.

This change began the fall I dug up a strip of ground underneath the alcove windows and put in some daffodil and tulip bulbs. Planting them was an act of faith that I would be there in the spring to see them blossom. As I troweled the bulbs into the dark earth, I thought that unless I were faithful, someone else might enjoy their spring beauty. What I realized after the long, cold winter was that it did not matter whether I would be faithful; God would be faithful to me.

Even fidelity was a gift I could not, of myself, promise to God. This insight, initially unsettling, brought with it a new dimension of peace. For there was Someone who could and *would* be faithful to me. My life and my future were to be built on this solid rock rather than on the slippery mud of my own human frailty.

Another, more risky commitment to my future in Colt Run

was choosing to sink a significant amount of money into a reliable water system. When others warned me I could be investing in improvements I might not enjoy for long, I paused. And prayed.

This question was posed: "What will you be losing?" "Money, Lord." "Only money?" Somehow that fluid resource did not seem worth clinging to. If I were improving this place for someone else to use, well, so be it. In the meantime, I would try to be a good steward of the property temporarily entrusted to my care.

In true Appalachian style, I focused my energies and what resources I had on the front of the house. It was slow going when I had to rely on myself. It took me two years to get all the rusting stoves and old tires hauled off to the landfill.

I had been profoundly distressed when, during my first winter, I had discovered that there were at least two trash dumps on my land stocked with, among other items, a freezer, an old washer, a truck frame, and an iron bedstead complete with springs. Summer weeds had mercifully hidden them from my view.

If I had had the strength and the means to do it, I would gladly have carted the accumulation to a landfill. Alas, the nearest one was in the next county, an hour's drive away, and the cost of dumping there was exorbitant. One had to be wealthy to dispose of trash, I realized with some bitterness.

No wonder some neighbors planted flowers in old vehicles permanently ensconced in front yards. "Bury it or beautify it" seemed to be the working principle. Following their example, I transplanted a leafy shrub to disguise a cement-filled barrel immovably fixed at the edge of my yard.

And, of course, there was the ever-present mud. Nothing motivated me to action more strongly than my impatience with this pervasive nuisance. Gradually, through my years of co-existence with slippery red muck, I learned a crucial lesson.

115

Impatience was the worst possible defense I could employ. What mud required was care — care where I set my booted foot; care how I sited the woodpile; care when and if I would bring a car up the drive.

Mud also taught me to dream . . . of grass. Grass! All my efforts to implant something green in the surrounding mud were constantly being undone. Firewood to be split was dumped on my baby grass. Bulldozers and ditchdiggers tore up my yard when the well and septic system were installed. Muddy runoff from the high ridges washed away grass seed or gouged new channels across the lawn.

Stubbornly I reseeded, time after time. Gradually, enough grass took root to raise the happy problem of mowing it. After I was exhausted by my efforts to start a power mower, someone gave me a wonderful machine. It performed almost silently, it required minimum upkeep and no gasoline, and best of all, its reels turned as soon as I pushed it.

I studied the problem of the steep bank that threatened to bury the brick walk I had built across the mud to the wood-shed door. With the help of a friend, I terraced it with land-scaping timbers and planted impatiens, whose bright colors lit up the shady spot.

The well I no longer used stood solidly in place before the kitchen window. One day I had a vision of it being roofed over with flowers blooming in a hanging bucket. I cajoled a visitor into constructing my dream from old two-by-fours, and lo, a picturesque "wishing well" graced my yard.

My efforts to transform a trashed cabin into a garden place brought me both satisfaction and frustration. Often, the Lord took over. One time, when I was gone for a few days, my sisters down the road constructed a deck by the front steps. What a joyous surprise! Then my ever-practical cousins came on the scene and built a screened porch over it. This not only gave me a mudroom in winter and a worship space

116

in warm weather but also permanently resolved the screen-door problem.

Someone who heard my sighs about the glorious rhododendrons that had graced my childhood home gave me a starter shrub. The balls of lavender blossoms were so breathtaking that even the meter man commented on their beauty. Lovingly I tended my shrub during its first summer, watering it, feeding it acid, ditching and mulching around it.

In early November, it was the only leafy bush left in the bleak landscape. And one terrible morning, it was no longer leafy. Foraging deer had ravaged it during the night. Hoping against hope, I left the stunted plant in place, and in the spring was cheered to see small shoots emerging from the roots and branches.

They soon wilted, however, for there was insufficient nurture to sustain them. All my prayers and care did not prevail, and one sad day, I pulled out the withered clump.

I learned to make hard choices and seize the moment (or hapless visitor!), addressing what tasks I could, and leaving larger concerns for God to manage. He did a glorious job in the fields, which produced a seasonal procession of wildflowers rivaling any planned garden I could dream of!

Working with the givens of my situation rather than trying to get rid of them became my mode of operation, partly because it was my only option. It was, after all, the way the Lord was working in me. He displayed an astonishing gentleness with my stubborn prejudices, my practiced deceptions, my secret comparisons, my endless ambitions.

I realized that even as I cherished a vision for my little place, so God had a dream for me. It included the very things I thought should have been pulled out, root and branch. My ambitions were transformed into energies by which I supported myself financially.

My habit of refusing to admit difficulties enabled me to

117

blindly undertake a life of poverty that a more foresighted person would have never attempted. And my secret desires to be different from others empowered me to become a solitary, adopting an irregular lifestyle seldom embraced in the twentieth century.

My prejudices were sharply challenged when I found that my moving outside the pale of the approved and acceptable subjected me to prejudice. For I had become threatening to the security and assumptions of those who had their own image of a religious, of a cloistered nun. Suddenly I was among the marginalized, the outcasts of secular and even religious culture.

I found myself in the company of many whom I had not accepted into my frame of reference before. Now we were one, we poor, we powerless and uneducated, we who lived invisibly on the fringes of American life. To my surprise, I found my new neighbors to be warm, generous, even humorous folks. No one in need went unaided by kin or neighbors. My pitiful prejudices crumbled.

Even my weaknesses and disadvantages were no obstacle for the Lord. I had no formal education beyond high school; my body was not robust; I had no financial resources. At fifty years of age, I had spent nearly two-thirds of my life in a cloistered community, so the "ways of the world" were largely unknown to me. But, as St. Paul had learned long before, "In weakness, [God's] power reaches perfection" (2 Cor. 12:9).

My single greatest asset was God's enduring love for me, which was revealed again and again as everything I needed (and more) fell providentially into my hands. Like grass seed . . . and bird feeders . . . and seed to fill them! I had always delighted in the melody of birdsong, and now, thanks to a special friend, my yard was alive with feathered friends whose calls, chirps, and whistles created a peaceful background to my prayer and work.

A hummingbird feeder at my kitchen window resembled

O'Hare International, with birds zooming in and out at a dizzying pace. During the winter months, a seed feeder attracted cardinals and chickadees and titmice — to the endless fascination of Merton, who lurked behind the curtain with lashing tail.

The God who cared for the birds of Colt Run and clothed with splendor the wildflowers in my field lavished attention on my every need and desire. I had often mused, as I sat on my porch, how delightful it would be to have an old-fashioned swing. And didn't some cousins turn up with a green porch swing a few months later?

As soon as warm weather returns, I will be swinging gently to the melody of birds and wind chimes, aware in the deepest part of my spirit that I am much loved, loved far beyond anything I could deserve or imagine. Being "worthy" does not seem so very important to God. Beyond all expectations, I've been given a small corner of Eden to tend in a state that has been nicknamed "Almost Heaven."

Yes, it is *almost* paradise. It still has its snakes and briars, its mud and trash. I do the little I can to heal a wounded land. And in the process I am learning to be patient. The ancient shed still rots slowly in my backyard. But someday it will be gone and replaced by a shady arbor. I know because I can dream it . . . and wait for it. There remain some unsightly features in my inner landscape, too, that the Lord has not yet transformed, but He is slowly, surely moving me closer to His dream for me.

A garden place grows slowly . . . not without muddy boots.

CPSIA information can be obtained
at www.ICGtesting.com
Printed in the USA
BVHW031327311220
596849BV00006B/54